# The Future of History

Socialist History 14

Edited by
Willie Thompson,
David Parker, Mike Waite,
David Morgan and
Heather Williams

Rivers Oram Press
London and New York

| Editorial Team | Editorial Advisors |
|---|---|
| Willie Thompson | Noreen Branson |
| David Parker | Rodney Hilton |
| Mike Waite | Eric Hobsbawm |
| David Morgan | David Howell |
| Heather Williams | Monty Johnstone |
| | Victor Kiernan |
| | David Marquand |
| | Kevin Morgan |
| | Ben Pimlott |
| | Pat Thane |

Published in 1999
by Rivers Oram Press, an imprint of Rivers Oram Publishers Ltd
144 Hemingford Road, London N1 1DE

Distributed in the USA by
New York University Press
Elmer Holmes Bobst Library
70 Washington Square South
New York, NY 10012-1091

Set in Garamond by
NJ Design Associates, Romsey, Hants
Printed and bound in Great Britain by
T. J. International Ltd.

This edition copyright © 1999 Socialist History Society
The articles are copyright © 1999 Richard Evans, Peter Jones, Brian Manning, Kevin Morgan, Mike Savage, Jim Sharpe, Roger Spalding, Eileen Yeo

No part of this journal may be produced in any form, except for the quotation of brief passages in criticism, without the written permission of the publishers. The right of the contributors to be identified as the authors has been asserted by them in accordance with the Copyright, Designs and Patents Act 1988

British Library Cataloguing in Publication Data
A catalogue record for this publication is available from the British Library
ISBN 1 85489 108 1 (hb)
ISBN 1 85489 109 X (pb)
ISSN 0969 4331

# Contents

**Editorial**

**History Today: Round-table dialogue**  1
Professor Jim Sharpe, Peter Jones, Mike Savage, Eileen Yeo, Kevin Morgan, Richard Evans

**The English Revolution: The decline and fall of**  40
**revisionism**
Brian Manning

**Popular Historiography in the Second World War**  54
A critique of J. Baxendale and C. Pawling, *Narrating The Thirties*
Roger Spalding

**Reviews**

*Culture and Imperialism*
Keith Ansell Pearson, Benita Parry and Judith Squires,
*Cultural Readings of Imperialism: Edward Said and the Gravity of History*
John Strawson  68

*The Challenges of Postmodernism*
John Belchem and Neville Kird (eds), *Languages of Labour;*
Ellen Meiksins Wood and John Bellamy Foster (eds), *In Defense of History: Marxism and the postmodern agenda*
Mike Waite  71

*Communist Historiography*
Noreen Branson, *History of the Communist Party of Great Britain
1941–1951*; Richard Pipes (ed.), *The Unknown Lenin: From the secret archive*;
Neil Harding, *Leninism*; Margarita Tupitsyn, *The Soviet Photograph
1924–1937*
Monty Johnson, Steven Fielding, H.C.A. Hughes                    **75**

*Versailles and Modernity*
David Parker, *Class and State in Ancien Régime France: The road to
modernity*
Donald Lowndes Sanderson                                          **82**

*Experiments with Extremes*
Momme Brodersen, *Walter Benjamin: A biography*; Gerhard Fischer (ed.),
*With the Sharpened Axe of Reason: Approaches to Walter Benjamin*
Sean Homer, Rosemary Bechler                                      **85**

*The Contest for Social Science*
Eileen Janes Yeo, *The Contest for Social Science: Relations and representations
of gender and class*
Karen Triggs                                                      **90**

*The Democracy of the Agents Themselves*
Colin Barker and Paul Kennedy (eds), *To Make Another World: Studies in
protest and collective action*
Laurence Cox                                                      **93**

*Valiant-for-Truth*
Peter Gathercole, T.H. Irving and Gregory Melleuish (eds), *Childe and
Australia: Archaeology, politics and ideas*
H.G.A. Hughes                                                     **96**

**Books Received**                                                **99**
**Correspondence**                                                **101**

# Editorial

No. 8 of *Socialist History* concentrated upon the British Marxist historians and their impact upon the course of historical studies in the UK and beyond. Our current number returns to the historiographical theme, but this time in a wider perspective. We consider and debate in this issue a number of issues relevant to the state of historical studies and public perceptions of these in Britain at the present time.

History, perhaps more than any other department of knowledge, exists both as an academic (or scientific) discipline and an area of significant public interest and concern. It is not rare for an academic text in this field to become a best-seller and of course the bookshops and book clubs are full of volumes of pop history with no pretensions to academic credibility but which return acceptable profits. History can also have directly political functions, occasionally commendable, but generally of a pretty disreputable sort — especially when historical myths of the nation or community are employed to generate hatred for outsiders. As Eric Hobsbawm has recently commented, 'The sentences typed on apparently innocuous keyboards may be sentences of death.'[1]

The relation between history as an academic pursuit, with its apparatus of archives, libraries, teaching establishments, conferences, specialist publishers; and history as a presence in public consciousness, is a complex and ambiguous one and to which we will return. Our concern at present is with academic history (not using that term disparagingly); or rather the writing of history, historiography.

It is hard to dispute that, while there are probably more historians alive now than the sum of all those who have ever lived in the past, and while they go about their business steadily adding to the sum of human knowledge, there is present a sense of turning points. The best recent comparison is perhaps with the 1960s, when new forms of historical writing were breaking onto the scene, most importantly in the area of social history.

Marxist historians, both in Britain and elsewhere, were especially associated with the latter development, with E.P. Thompson's classic as its outstanding monument (though *The Making of the English Working Class* was much more than social history narrowly conceived). It can be argued that the present sense of new departures is partly due to the internal evolution of historical studies, the inherent logic of the concepts which the new social history brought to the fore — but also partly from the impact of historical realities in the last third of this century.

So far as the first is concerned, a focus upon social mentalities — recognisable as far back as Thompson's insistence that any concept of class (particularly the working class) has to include class consciousness — draws attention to language as the medium of consciousness and gives rise to the question as to whether historians can ever purport to understand the past outside the terms, language codes and outlook of the alien cultures (made alien by the passage of time) they try to investigate. In other words, is it possible to make universalistic judgments or import contemporary values into our accounts of past realities? In considering this we are already on the ground of postmodernism.

As for the impact of current realities, it is easy enough to observe that the debacle of both communism and social democracy[2] has meant the loss for historians of the 'grand narratives', the implied presumption of an historical progress and ultimate destination for society, which provided the taken-for-granted framework, the perspective, often unconscious, of their historiographical endeavours, even when they consciously maintained that historical events were nothing more the 'one damned thing after another'.

E.H. Carr in the 1960s wrote that whatever their formal political allegiances, the overwhelming majority of English historians were liberals in their essential outlook. He might have said 'western historians' and 'social democrats' in that what was meant was the implicit belief at the time that, after millennia of blood and tears climaxing in the 1940s, the secret of indefinite improvement and progress had been arrived at at last, and that (barring nuclear catastrophe) humanity would continue down this route into the indefinite future.[3] Marxist historians shared these presumptions (and more consciously) in essence if not in detail. Now, the intellectual climate is completely different and the twenty-first century looks a lot more like a threat than a promise. Taking all these things together it is hardly surprising that there should be some crisis of confidence in certain areas of the profession.

The arrival of the postmodern challenge[4] in historiography is one expression of that crisis: which is not to make any prejudgement on the validity or otherwise of postmodernism — Minerva's owl may well fly at dusk (or it may stay on its perch). Another is the sign of a gap opening up between academic and popular historiography (reflected in a minor way in the deteriorating quality of the the texts offered in the historical book clubs). The comments of David Cannadine on this relationship are interesting, particularly given his status as an academic historian who has achieved near-bestseller status. He notes that: 'the view of the world projected by today's media lacks temporal perspective and is excessively sensationalised, trivialised, personalised .... the present Labour government projects an image of not being concerned with the past .... except insofar as it wants to get rid of it'.[5]

The contemporary debate in historiography ismore far-reaching than that of the 1960s in that there now exist disagreement among historians as to what is meant by the concept of history, greatly transcending previous disputes regarding its content. *Socialist History*, from its own specific position, attempts to contribute to that dialogue.

## Content of No.14

The largest part of this volume is taken up with a Roundtable discussion on Revisionism and Postmodernism and their impact on historical study and writing. This discussion was intended to fulfil a number of purposes. One was to give some explicit consideration to theoretical and historiographical questions which over the years have played only a minimal part in the publications and events sponsored by our Society and its predecessor. The progress made in recent years by revisionist and postmodernist tendencies together with the collapse of communism in eastern Europe means that it is not possible any longer to simply assume that there exists a shared but unspoken nexus of interpretations and ideas which binds Marxist or leftish historical thinking together. In this context the purpose of the Roundtable was simply to stimulate a considered assessment of the current historiographical agenda. In doing so it seemed important to avoid two potential traps. One would have been to set up an unproductive confrontation between the most strident defenders of Postmodernism and its critics. We hope that readers will agree that the resulting discussion vindicates this approach by offering a starting point for reflection about Postmodernism which is both informative and considered. More difficult was the question of what attention to give Marxism, about which it has been virtually impossible to stimulate serious discussion since 1989. The polarisation between those who overnight effectively abandoned Marxism and those who retreated further into a vulgarised view of the onward march of history has so far left little space for constructive debate. It was not therefore intended that the Roundtable should engage in the easy pastime of knocking down vulgarised versions of Marxist history, nor be a form of confessional for the expiation of past errors. On the other hand, the intention was not to resurrect old teleologies which, in any event, have long ceased to be significant features of Marxist historiography. Although, as readers will see, the discussion did not dissipate all anxieties on this score it did generate an exchange of views which was both critical and constructive. The space for discussion about the continuing relevance of Marxism will certainly grow as the anguish and disorientation of the Left provoked by the events of 1989 gives way to the need to address the problems posed by capitalism's triumphs and disasters.

What united the participants and made the discussion possible despite significant differences in approach and emphasis, was a shared belief that the study of history can be both committed and scholarly. The willingness of eminent specialists to participate is noteworthy. The sole practical restraint in bringing together a panel was the small number of professional women historians in many fields of study.

The printed version of the discussion replicates the words that were uttered and the sense of what was said has been retained throughout. Nevertheless it proved necessary to edit where several participants were talking at once, to eliminate hesitations and choose between different formulations where participants repeated themselves. The conversational style has been retained as far as possible but there were moments at which this translated badly into the written word without additional punctuation or some rephrasing. It is hoped that it will be possible to make the tape generally available for those who wish to pick up more closely.

The two articles which follow address issues and arguments in British historiography concerning two crucial turning points in the country's development, the sixteenth-century revolution and the Second World War. These are followed by a number of reviews, most of them relating to the historiographical theme.

## Socialist History

We would like once again to thank readers for their patience in the course of 1998 while waiting for the appearance of No.13. With this number it can be seen that the problems of last year are now fully overcome and that the journal will be resuming its full service to Society members and to its wider readership. Some particularly fascinating themes are in prospect — they include 'The History of the Future', and the question of 'The American Century — Yes or No?' Readers who would like to advance suggestions are encouraged to contact the editor.

**The Editors**

## Notes

1. *On History* (London, 1997) p.277.
2. Although parties still operating under these names continue to exist and may even be in office it is clear that their contemporary programmes bear little or no resemblance to what has been understood hitherto as either communism or social democracy.
3. Most explicitly propounded in C.A.R. Crosland's *The Future of Socialism*.
4. See Patrick Joyce, 'The Return of History: Postmodernism and the Politics of Academic History in Britain', *Past & Present*, No.158, February 1998
5. *History Today*, Vol.40, No.10, October 1998, p.26.

# Socialist History Journal

The *Socialist History Journal* explores and assesses the past of the socialist movement and broader processes in relation to it, not only for the sake of historical understanding, but as an input and contribution to the movement's future development. The journal is not exclusive and welcomes argument and debate from all viewpoints.

## Other *Socialist History* titles:

A Bourgeois Revolution?
*Socialist History 1 · 1993*
0 7453 08058

What Was Communism? Pt 1
*Socialist History 2 · 1993*
0 7453 08066

What Was Communism? Pt 2
*Socialist History 3 · 1993*
0 7453 08074

The Labour Party Since 1945
*Socialist History 4 · 1994*
0 7453 08082

The Left and Culture
*Socialist History 5 · 1994*
0 7453 08090

The Personal and the Political
*Socialist History 6 · 1994*
0 7453 08104

Fighting the Good Fight?
*Socialist History 7 · 1995*
0 7453 10613

Historiography and the British Marxist Historians
*Socialist History 8 · 1995*
0 7453 08120

Labour Movements
*Socialist History 9 · 1996*
0 7453 08139

Revisions?
*Socialist History 10 · 1996*
0 7453 08147

The Cold War
*Socialist History 11 · 1997*
0 7453 12411

Nationalism and Communist Party History
*Socialist History 12 · 1997*
0 7453 12675

Imperialism and Internationalism
*Socialist History 13 · 1998*
1 85489 1073

The Future of History
*Socialist History 14 · 1998*
1 85489 1154

Visions of the Future
*Socialist History 15 · 1999*
1 85489 115 4

America
*Socialist History 16 · 1999*
1 85489 117 0

# History Today
Round-table dialogue

The following discussion was recorded in the Media Studies Studio at the University of Leeds on the 18 June 1998. It was devised and chaired by David Parker, one of the editors of *Socialist History*. Those taking part were, in broadly chronological order:

**Professor Jim Sharpe** a social historian of seventeenth century England at the Department of History, York University; he has published particularly on crime and, more recently, witchcraft.

**Peter Jones** Professor of History at Birmingham a specialist of France in the late eighteenth century whose recent publications include a major study of the French peasantry during the revolution and another on the passage from reform to revolution.

**Mike Savage** Professor of Sociology at Manchester University, after spells at North Carolina, Keele and Surrey, is a historical sociologist and social theorist who has worked on class relations in British History and the history of bureaucracy.

**Eileen Yeo** Reader in History at Sussex, has written extensively on class and gender issues in Britain and is now undertaking a comparative book, *Meanings of Motherhood in Europe and America 1750 to the Present*. She has been a major presence in the Society for the Study of Labour History.

**Kevin Morgan** Lecturer in Government at Manchester, his research interests lie in the twentieth century, particularly British labour and social history and comparative communist politics. He is writing a book on Bolshevism and the British Left.

**Richard Evans** has recently completed his move from Birkbeck to Cambridge as Professor of Modern History. He is well known for his work on modern German history and his recent book, *In Defence of History*, attracted much attention and was very relevant to the discussion.[1]

## Revisionism and postmodernism

**David Parker** This discussion is about the effects of revisionist and postmodernist tendencies on our view of history and the way it is practised. I want to begin by postulating a view of the historical discipline that is, I think, broadly shared by all of those present. It rests on the conviction that the discipline of the historian is sufficiently rigorous to enable us to interpret the past with a degree of confidence and that we can, to paraphrase the concluding words of Richard's recent book, find out what happened in the past, how it happened, and to reach some conclusions — albeit never final — about what it all meant.

The conviction that history has a meaning has not just been a feature of marxisant or leftish historians. Since the Enlightenment the notion that history is a narrative of human progress or emancipation has had a powerful — if not totally unchallenged — hold on the assumptions of a wide swathe of liberal, as well as leftish, historians.

Despite disagreements about precise causes and outcomes, there has been a surprising degree of consensus about what are the major landmarks in the unfolding story, whether it has been described in Whiggish or Marxist terms or simply as a process of modernisation. These landmarks have included the English and French Revolutions, the industrial revolution, the development of class in its modern forms together with the emergence of a mature labour movement, the Russian Revolution and the formation of the modern state.

Over the last two or three decades practically every one of the assumptions that has gone into this conception has been under sustained criticism at different levels. At the more immediately historical level, revisionist historians have sought to reduce or even demolish the significance of these landmarks. More latterly, the very idea that the past is knowable, that there is a grand narrative, or any meaning apart from the historian's subjective reading of the story and the texts on which it is based, has been challenged by the postmodernist insistence on the fragmentary and the particular.

I would like, in the first part of our discussion, to deal with revisionism in order to see how much of the narrative you think intact. We might begin by asking Jim and Peter how much of the traditional — and here I am using shorthand — liberal-Marxist consensus about the English and French Revolutions they think is left and how much is irrecoverable.

## Revisionism and the 'bourgeois' revolutions

**Jim Sharpe** It is fair to say that recent thinking on the English Revolution — which is more likely to be referred to as the English Civil War, or the British Civil Wars these days — has been marked by a massive reassessment of the causation of those events and by a retreat from what was the prevailing model when I was an undergraduate thirty years ago — a socio-economic explanation of what happened, which was attached to the notion of the transition from feudalism to capitalism and which would see the English Civil War as a product of a rising bourgeois revolution; or, as it was reformulated in light of comments by Tawney in 1941, the idea that the motor — the class motor if you like — of the English Revolution was the gentry who cropped up as a bourgeoisie of convenience in writing around the middle years of this century.[2] The concentration now is much more on the importance of short term causes. The outbreak of the war is seen as the result of Charles I's ineptitude and a run of bad luck which brings in the British dimensions of the Scottish rebellion of 1637 and the Irish rebellion of 1641 and which wrecked the possibility of a consensus between Charles I and his subjects. I would say that the early stages of the war and the political crisis of 1640–2 looks more like a rerun of King John and the barons than it does a picture of a rising bourgeoisie. The big problem is that the English Civil War has been studied too much from the modern end without taking medieval history into account.

**DP** So the bourgeois revolution completely disappears?

**JS** Yes.

**DP** And you think we have to live with that?

**JS** Something changed between 1500 and 1800. There was a developing bourgeoisie in England, but the idea that what happened in the middle decades of the seventeenth century was a bourgeois revolution is not sustainable. We are looking at shifting patterns of relationships between central authority and élites — an English version of what is going on in continental Europe.

**DP** Peter, what do you think? Are we in the same sort of position with the French Revolution?

**Peter Jones** No. We are perhaps a little further advanced down the road of historiographical reappraisal in as much as we have had an orthodox interpretation, we have had revisionism and arguably we now have post-revisionism. So what I would like to do is sketch the respective positions which have unfolded over the last few decades. These are labels, of course, and they are both useful and tricky. They tend to gather up developments and trends and freeze dry them, and it is then very difficult to disentangle and restore the dynamism of events once they have been labelled orthodox, revisionist and so on.

With that caveat, I would say that we have moved from an orthodox position which still largely obtained when I was a student at this university.[3] This was a view of the revolution which was neo-Jacobin, not to say Marxist, a view which was crystallised at the end of the nineteenth century when a republican historiography was anxious to annex the revolution as its birthright and rescue it from clericalist, royalist and other interpretations. So we started with the republican interpretation which I have dubbed 'orthodox', but that went through a number of gestational changes. Before long it acquired a social and economic underpinning; and then, in due course, what I would call a non-doctrinal socialist underpinning — that would take us into the 1900s, 1910s and the name to cite here would be that of Jean Jaurès. Then, with the Red Dawn of 1917, we get the full-blown doctrinal Marxist interpretation of the revolution. It was in that orthodox form that it was handed on as a precious commodity into my undergraduate days.

But I would stress that there was some movement even within that so called Marxist interpretation. I need cite only two examples: Lefèbvre, the great French historian, altered the inheritance that he received, in as much as he discovered a peasant revolution which did not fit neatly into the classical Marxist version.[4] And so during the 1920s and 1930s there was a bit of pushing and shoving to fit this peasant revolution in, and Lefèbvre was criticised by the Communist faithful. Albert Soboul, who is often regarded as the great Marxist exponent of the French Revolution, also encountered resistance in those early days following his discovery of the revolution of the *sans culottes*.[5] The Marxist tradition at that time did not allow for anything to the left of the bourgeoisie. Therefore he, too, was criticised before his research was admitted into the Marxian pantheon. Then, in more recent times, we have had Leninist perspectives brought to bear on the revolution, whether it be applied to the *sans culottes* or to the peasantry.[6]

What about revisionism? I think revisionism begins to be detectable from the late 1960s and it focuses initially on all these givens, which although they had some flexibility were largely referred to as givens. What drove it? It's difficult to say but a mixture, I think, of anti-communism and intellectual doubt. The revisionists focused initially on the marxian social interpretation of the French Revolution, the notion of a transition from feudalism to capitalism and the idea of a bourgeois revolution as then understood, and so on. But then, I think, the revisionists moved off these targets and began to launch a general assault on all social interpretations of the French Revolution. The man who most neatly captured this shift was an American historian George V. Taylor who argued that the 1789 was 'essentially a political revolution with social consequences and not a social revolution with political consequences'.[7] Once the social and socialist interpretations had been cleared out of the way all manner of things were unleashed under the general rubric of revisionism. Ideas, intellectual history, which had not found much space in French Revolution historiography were unleashed; there was room, too, for a gendered interpretation of the French Revolution. Once class was cleared out of the way, gender became a real opportunity for revisionist historians.

What have the casualties been? I would say that class has been a casualty certainly, and also capitalism. But more worrying for me has been the major casualty: causality. We have lost our clear understanding of the causes of 1789. Another casualty is our understanding of the enlightenment as in some sense spearheaded by the bourgeoisie.

**DP** So both of you are really wilting before this revisionist storm. Can I just ask whether you can retain something of the notion of the transition from feudalism to capitalism and the eventual triumph of the bourgeoisie, even if these revolutionary moments no longer constitute a central rupture?

**JS** I was fascinated listening to that account of the historiography of the French Revolution because, frankly, the generality of historians working on these big things in seventeenth-century England are not willing to confront that sort of theory. There has only been one major Marxist thinker working on the seventeenth century within the recent past — Christopher Hill, a man whose work, whilst respected, has not attracted a large school. So these successive Marxist interpretations, which have been directed to the French Revolution have not, I think, been so strong in the case of seventeenth-century England.

Just a couple of other points. One is of course that things did change, although the early stages of the English Revolution can be interpreted, as in the case of the French Revolution, as a break in the ruling class. This is a very familiar seventeenth-century theme: a privileged ruling class increasingly annoyed by an innovatory, centralising government. I think this is the problem in 1642. But after the war has been going on for a couple of years, and certainly after peace comes and after the execution of Charles I, one can see social groupings coming on to the political arena in ways that they had not done previously; with the Leveller movement which has not been much studied recently you begin to see something, which although not quite the *sans culottes* is a self consciously popular political movement, basically *petit bourgeois* I think, but one which is new. The English economy also explodes after mid century; I think it would have done so without the English Revolution but one obviously confronts problems of economic change, social change and class formation; and the class being formed is the bourgeoisie.

So, if one looks at overall developments, one can see what could be described as a transition from feudalism to capitalism taking place. But there are two major problems. First, there is the question of how far the events across the middle of the century, which we know as the English Revolution actually furthered those developments or how far those developments would have taken place without them. Second, current orthodoxy, whilst accepting a developing bourgeois presence which is finally going to establish itself as a voice in 1832, lays tremendous stress on the continuing aristocratic domination of British society even beyond that date. So a transition was taking place, but this was slower and less definite than historians would have thought, say, a generation ago.

**DP** It seems to me that, whilst you are saying that there are some real historical problems of interpretation, the language you are using is quite interesting; you are talking about a *petite bourgeoisie*, you are talking about an aristocracy, you are still using the traditional language of class. If one inserts into this, as Peter did, the lower orders, that still, it seems to me, doesn't, in the end, detract from the global view. Christopher Hill has long said that there were two revolutions: one was a successful bourgeois one and one was an unsuccessful popular one. And if you then add the other element which you both did — and which, I think, is absolutely vital — that is the fissures within the ruling classes or élites, I myself have no problem as Marxist with that.

**JS** I do find myself much more attracted to traditional terminology than some other historians. The problem is — and this is perhaps going back to the low level of theorisation on English social structures to use another old-fashioned term — that there are tremendous problems in using the concept of class in pre-industrial society. Although I am happy to use terms like bourgeoisie or aristocracy as categories which are generally accepted and generally understood, the real problems begin when on tries to place categories on social groupings beneath the bourgeoisie. I think it is very difficult to talk about the working class in seventeenth-century England.

**DP** I would like to ask for comments about where the industrial revolution fits. Before I do that may I just ask you a fairly blunt question. Do you think — and I have the impression from your comments about 1832 that you do not — that the bourgeoisie was in power by the early eighteenth century; and do you, Peter, think the French bourgeoisie was in power by the early nineteenth century regardless of all these qualifications?

**PJ** Yes I do, but I think we have redefined the bourgeoisie. We have stripped it of its materialist base. To go back to your original question we can retrieve the bourgeois revolution as long as we redefine it but I am not sure that in the French case we can retrieve the transition from feudalism to capitalism.

**DP** So which is the aspect of the bourgeoisie which has been lost?

**PJ** We would have to start defining it in more culturalist terms and we would have to question whether it can be linked to any sort of laissez-faire vision. It could be that the French bourgeoisie emerges from the revolution with a corporatist vision and not into an environment free for capitalism as it were, as it used to be argued. 1789 takes place, feudalism is cleared out of the way, a new environment comes into being with its new social embodiment, the bourgeoisie: I'm not so sure we can keep that.

**DP** But if we redefine the bourgeoisie in cultural terms then you are saying we cam still make a case for it being dominant by the early nineteenth century. Now Jim, you were almost going with Jonathan Clark — England's *ancien régime* lasts until 1832?[8]

**JS** Yes. I'm sorry about that. I read Jonathan Clark after I had formed a lot of my opinions on these broad themes and felt with a sinking sense of dismay that I agreed with a lot of it. There is an obviously increasing bourgeois presence. One thinks of John Smail's recent book on Halifax in the eighteenth century where he traces a growing middle-class, bourgeois presence.[9] This was a cultural, as well as an economic presence, in the mid-eighteenth century; but, despite this, England over most of the eighteenth century is basically an aristocratic dominated society with an increasing bourgeois commercial interest, coexisting for the most part quite happily with the aristocracy.

**DP** But there is an aggressive commercial foreign policy which is in my terms very bourgeois, there is a financial revolution which has long been understood which is very bourgeois, and arguably large chunks of the landed classes are bourgeois.

**JS** Well obviously one of the key issues all the way through — with the bourgeoisie buying into land, especially if they take titles — is how you categorise them socially. You can also put forward a strong case for saying that the financial revolution is essentially a product, as it begins in the late seventeenth century, of the ruling class deciding that they want William and Mary to be their joint monarchs rather than James II. They get Protestantism and the maintenance of social hierarchy, William of Orange gets the resources of the English state to fight Louis XIV. I think it is at that stage .... that one can see a quickening of financial relationships in England which obviously involve people with financial expertise, many of whom are imported from outside, but which is essentially driven by that foreign policy rather than forces within English society.

**DP** Now people like Clark have been much sustained by some of the revisionist work around the industrial revolution and I was just wondering, Mike, having listened to that discussion, particularly that last bit about whether we are still in an *ancien régime* in eighteenth century England, where you feel we are left with the work on the industrial revolution.

## Industrial Revolution

**Mike Savage** Well, I think it's interesting to compare the industrial revolution with the French and English Revolutions because, of course, the term has always been contested and because there are no obvious events which you can hang a story round; the very idea of the industrial revolution has always been more difficult to make into the key orthodoxy. And, I think, you can argue that it is really only in the 1950s and 1960s with the emergence of a kind of social science history that the term becomes really canonised in British research. But I am also struck, in the context of this discussion about revisionism, that you can actually argue, in the case of the industrial revolution, that revisionism arrives early. The mechanist socio-economic determinist view of the industrial revolution came with the American sociologists Smelser and Parsons and modernisation theory in the 1950s and then you get the first attempt to present a more culturalist approach with E.P. Thompson in the early 1960s.[10] What has happened since that period is the elaboration of a kind of pluralist set of positions which do suggest that reductionist, economistically driven notions of the industrial revolution are problematic, whilst at the same time hanging on to the idea that this was a period of profound social disruption.

Some historians have gone back in time, particularly with the debate about proto-industrialisation and found the roots of industry in earlier and earlier periods. In a sense, the discussion has gone right back to the debate about feudalism and capitalism, particularly with the work around Brenner in the seventies.[11] So in some respects some historians have gone back in time but what has also happened is that key changes have been pushed towards the present day with debates about the persistence of the agrarian aristocratic classes until the end of the Victorian period or early twentieth century. The work of Rubinstein and Cannadine has shown the persistence of agrarian rule and aristocratic classes in British society right down to the first world war.[12] So, in some ways, the notion of a transition has been stretched out and we now have a multiple picture of smaller scale transitions. That having been said, the notion of a formative period of British society being the early nineteenth century which is obviously one of the key features of E.P. Thompson's work, remains; and I am struck, as someone who has engaged with this for much of my professional life and has been critical of aspects of it, by the idea which he presents of a key moment in the development of the British polity and the way in which the working class entered politics and played a key role in defining notions of democracy and citizenship.

If I can leap to my sociological work, I have been interviewing people around Manchester. One of the peculiar idiosyncrasies of Britain is that, in a service-sector-dominated economy where many people do managerial professional white collar work, if you ask people to identify what class they belong to two thirds of people still say they are working class. In Japan 90 per cent of people say they are middle class, in the US it's about two thirds, in Europe it's more varied. But in Britain, amazingly enough, in a massively tertiarised white collar labour market, the notion of the working class and the idea of the working class having some kind of democratic clout does have some persistence. This, can be traced back — I think Thompson was right — to the historical ferment of the early part of the nineteenth century. Obviously important changes have taken place since then but I do think there is something there which we should not lose sight of.

**Eileen Yeo** I quite agree, Mike, that the whole concept of the industrial revolution has been a very contested one from the very time that this epochal process was supposed to be at its height. Back in the 1820s and 1830s it was acknowledged by people at the time that something very fundamental was happening but the way they characterised that happening and the way they evaluated it varied greatly. It is interesting that the argument has resonated ever since and keeps recurring. On the one hand, you had political economists and Utilitarians who were singing paeans of praise to national economic growth and production of a very narrowly defined type of wealth. On the other hand, you had cooperative economists and socialists who said, as did Robert Owen, that 'this revolution would bring about a greater change than all the previous revolutions which have agitated the world'. But what they said was that you had to measure happiness by the physical, mental and moral well being of the great majority, namely the working classes or 'the people' to whom we have just referred. And their verdict was that a new technology was being employed within a competitive system of social relations which brought to the great majority insecurity, redundancy and the threat of incarceration in the workhouse.

This whole business of whether the experience was a positive one to be seen in terms of economic growth and modernisation or an immiserating one to be seen in terms of decline in the quality and standard of life for the majority of the population has run and run. It had another moment when the Hammonds were fighting Clapham a hundred years later in the 1920s; and then when I was graduate student in the 1960s we had Hartwell versus Hobsbawm in the standard of living controversy.[13] Everybody in those various moments of engagement did acknowledge that something quite important had happened between 1780 and 1850 in British society, however they cared to configure it. I suppose the more recent revisionists are saying that frankly nothing spectacular happened from the point of view of national growth rates which were much slower than we had ever thought. I do not accept that as a reason for dismissing fundamental change in the period.

**DP** But you all seem so far in the discussion to be stretching out this transition. Does this mean we are left without our revolutionary moments? You are happy to talk in terms of class, you are happy to talk in terms of feudalism and capitalism...

**EY** The industrial revolution, even if I would not want to call it that, was a moment of rupture. It was a crisis — an economic political, social and cultural crisis which made the early nineteenth century a time of profound realignment in social relations. I don't know if you want me to gloss any further?

**DP** I'm interested in trying to work out what you think is left of older views. The impression I'm getting is that although you have made a qualification you are happy, and Jim was clearly very happy, to use the traditional structural language. Most people are, but they have revised their picture of the processes.

## Cultural perspectives and historical change

**Richard Evans** It is quite clear that something big happens when the monarchy in the eighteenth or mid seventeenth century is overthrown and replaced by a republic — a lot of people get killed, the constitution is changed, lots of new ideas come about; it is quite clear that something big is happening, when irrespective of rates of growth in the economy, you get transition to the use of steam and coal power, the whole nature of power as a resource begins to change. I don't think that anybody looking at it in the global perspective would challenge the assertion that these are major events which need explaining. What seems to me to have happened is that they are no longer explained as the outcome of class struggles. Marx's dictum that all history is the history of class struggle has now effectively gone. There are few professional historians who will use that concept as a way of explaining events and processes such as these. So we need to distinguish between what needs explaining and how we explain it.

There is a broader development which is that, in the place of class struggle, there isn't just confusion but a distinct movement now which one can broadly call postmodernist or post-structuralist. This tries to look at culture — political culture, culture in a broader sense, and the ideas, assumptions and ideologies of societies — the word discourse comes to mind — as a way of, if not explaining these things, at least of understanding them. I think that you will find that a lot of younger historians, particularly in the United States, are looking at things like the French Revolution — and we can mention Keith Baker and people whom he has influenced — in terms of the political culture.[14] Tony Wrigley — though he's not a younger historian — recently wrote about industrialisation in terms of cultural determinants.[15] So that the whole idea that many historians, particularly on the Left, used to have that we had politics and culture at the 'top' and you explain the changes by going 'down' to look at the economy and society changing — that has all not just been jettisoned but actually turned on its head.

**DP** And you are discarding class along with that? Or at least a structural definition of class. Kevin, you were nodding then.

**Kevin Morgan** You were asking whether we can talk about capitalism, whether we can talk about feudalism. In a sense the missing element of your trilogy was socialism. You used the phrase a narrative of human progress — almost a teleological view. The sense that this teleology has not worked out has a created part of the context in which, directly as a consequence of the declining credibility of the French left, of the French Communist party and of French Marxism, you get some of these revisionist approaches to the French Revolution. Look at someone like François Furet.[16] It is the same thing in a British context. It is notoriously said of very eminent Communist Party historians that they were not able or did not attempt to engage with twentieth century history. They engaged in very creative ways with the transition from feudalism to capitalism and the early nineteenth century but there was no comparable scholarship on twentieth century Britain or Europe.

And I would even say, that Marxist historical scholarship of the twentieth century was far richer in terms of movements of the right, of Nazism (people like Blackburn, Eley and so on),[17] than it was in relation to the actual agencies and moments of social transformation. In a sense that part of the equation never worked out. It strikes me that, in relation to twentieth century history, the notion of a narrative of human progress or emancipation has never actually had the standing of a consensus.

**RE** Well its very difficult to see a lot of twentieth-century history in terms of human emancipation and progress.

**KM** Except by writing out a hell of a lot of people who were obviously not part of that equation.

**RE** Can I just make a further point which is that, it seems to me, that a lot of this is connected with changing social structure and changing social cleavages and changing agendas on the left. What we are talking about here are not the familiar landmarks which all historians in Europe and America have always adhered to. They are specifically landmarks of a specifically left-wing and socialist history and as you have already heard all these arguments about the economic and social determination — and even the label — of the English Revolution or the French Revolution — these have all been very contested from the centre and the right, from the very beginning. What is seems to me to be happening is a crisis among historians who think of themselves of being broadly on the Left. And here we are living at the very end of the twentieth century when you can no longer say that the industrial working class is the vehicle of social and political progress; on the contrary it is declining in many different ways. Other social cleavages and social divisions are becoming just as important as that kind of class division — we have gender, sexual orientation and, whether you like it or not, religion in many parts of the world — all these things are different ways of looking at society and many can be conceptualised in terms of culture and it seems to me that what it is to be on the Left is now something very different from what it was twenty or thirty forty years ago. It therefore follows that if you are a historian on the Left that you will look at history in a different way. In many ways this is very liberating. One of the troubles I have with the agenda as you sketched it out the beginning, David, is that you are repeating the old E.H. Carr view that history is not interesting until the eighteenth century, and after that the only people who are interesting are those who have contributed to a model of progress which ends up with a Soviet-style planned economy; the mass of people are not interesting until they join the labour movement and you are consigning the vast majority of people in history to the famous dust-heap.

If we look at history in terms of these other kinds of cleavages, they become much more important — we can look and learn lessons from and talk and write about people who lived in completely different situations and different cultures a thousand or two thousand years ago. We don't just have to stick to the modern version of history which you sketched out.

**DP** Well, I think, you have read an awful lot into what I said! But I just want to go back to the first comment you made about it being only a history of the Left — this modernising, progressive emancipatory sort of thing which I sketched in very briefly at the beginning. Because there is a Whig version of the English Revolution, unfolding of democracy; the French Revolution has also been incorporated into that scenario as the early nineteenth French liberal historians had a view not only of themselves of as the heirs of a bourgeois liberal revolution but of a progressive evolution of the French state, a powerful notion.

**PJ** But, David, they were the Left of their day.

**RE** Also David, I would concede that coming from a background of working on German history I look at what German historians over the years — until the 1960s — were writing about the French Revolution. Of course it was overwhelmingly negative. You have historiographies in Europe which are overwhelmingly right-wing and even in terms of the French Revolution you have a strongly right-wing historiography — from Taine and before; I guess that never disappeared.

**DP** This is a true; any historical set of propositions is always contested. I still think that I would argue that history since the Enlightenment has been presented as a story of progress — despite the irruptions of those who intervened to say that it doesn't mean anything at all and that it's one damn fact after another. The notion of it going somewhere is something that has been shared by more than the Left.

**JS** I do take the point that Whigs in the mid nineteenth century could be portrayed as the Left of the day but this notion is absolutely central to what we call the Whig interpretation. It is one of those little ironies that Macaulay wrote volume one of his history of England in 1848, the same year that the Communist Manifesto came out.

One thing I would like to contest, though, with Richard is the jettisoning of notions of class. Although there are obviously problems about using the terms for pre-industrial periods, before 1750 or 1800, and we do have wonderful things like gender to worry about, I do think that people's positions in the social hierarchy is something which conditions their experience. If one revisits the very traditional field of study of élite politics in any period, and certainly in the period with which I am most familiar, one of the things that is now apparent is the way in which a lot of what is happening at the top of society is to do with deals being struck between central authority and people in élite positions. I don't think that, in the broad sense, you can rule class out of history. I don't accept that all history was the history of class struggles because it manifestly wasn't, but I do think there are certain areas where the problems which, I think, Lenin characterised as 'who and whom' — who is actually wielding power, how power is operating — are still very important ones. A couple of years ago I was teaching a seminar in Yorkshire to undergraduates and I was talking about the 'cobbling together' of the Tudor state and the Tudor monarchs doing deals with the nobility and local urban élites. One of my students turned to me, somewhat sneeringly, and said that sounds very Marxist. And I said yes it does; you can't escape things from these things entirely.

**DP** Very quickly as I want to bring Eileen in on this ...

**RE** Okay, as I am sure Eileen has got more to say about this than I have; but one of the biggest 'who and whom' questions is to do with men and women, 50 per cent each of society, roughly. Feminist historians might ask perfectly legitimately what has the question of the oppression of women in any given society got do to do with the events like the French and English revolutions — do they matter when you look at history in that way?

**EY** Well they do. Feminist historians precisely looking at the French Revolution have spent a lot of time reviewing the discrepancy between the promise of the universalism of the rhetoric of that revolution and the partial actualisation of those promises with certain very obvious groups left out, like women.

**RE** It doesn't matter in fact. It doesn't make that much difference.

**EY** It does, because women wanted to get in on the act. As that promise was now available, it became a matter of how to negotiate a way into the public sphere both in France and Britain; and for most women, how to negotiate in a way that allowed them to remain respectable and credible. This opens up a very interesting area for historical analysis. Far from junking the French Revolution or saying that the demands that the Chartists were making are discredited, both historical women and women scholars want to know why those promises were kept restricted to men and how women tried to fight into a larger space.[18]

**RE** Sure. I accept that, but they are not milestones on the road of progress for women are they?

**EY** But that's not the way we look at history as feminist historians. It's not a heroic progressive history. It's about how we live and struggle within constructs of femininity, and masculinity, and how we try to bring about change. Struggle has always been problematic for women and is still a complicated business.

**PJ** I simply want to say that I wonder whether feminist historians are not assuming rather a lot when they analyse and dissect and condemn the male French revolutionaries. They are assuming to start with that women participated in the French Revolution as women. But that's an assumption. We can't be sure of that. They might have been participating as Jacobins, or maybe as Royalists. Therefore we must not condemn anachronistically. We have got to be absolutely sure that there was an expanding space for women before 1789 which the revolutionaries then closed down in a masculine, deliberate fashion. I'm not persuaded that anything of the sort took place at all.

**EY** You are dubious, but there has been a lot of writing along these lines by feminist students of French history.

**PJ** All right, there were female Jacobin clubs that were closed down in late 1793, but they opened before they closed down and this seems to me to be highly significant. In how many revolutionary situations in that period, or in the seventeenth century did you have female political clubs?. How many Quaker women were able to organise into clubs in the 1640s?

**JS** The whole club thing would be anachronistic, I think, in that period. But I do take your point. There is evidence, particularly articulated through religious rhetoric or religious participation of involvement by women in the radical movement in or after the civil war but very little was formalised and it was regarded by most contemporaries who saw fit to pass their opinions as something rather odd and rather undesirable.

**MS** Can I just summarise ...?

**DP** This discussion has moved from class to gender and I do not want to lose sight of the question of how far you are going down Richard's road of saying that class has gone. Jim made it very clear that he thought we could retain something.

**RE** Well I wasn't saying that class has gone entirely. There are obviously some extreme postmodernist writers who would like to say that class is a mere concept, a discourse like any other that has no basis in reality. From my point of view it is a useful tool of analysis, but one amongst many. What we certainly cannot say and should not say is that it is the primary way of explaining historical change, even in the modern period.

## Class and power

**MS** I think what you are saying, and what we would all probably agree with, is that the idea that class as the kind of historical actor pushing the historical scripts forward has gone, that sense of historicism and class and class being the privileged actor driving history has gone. I do not think what we would necessarily agree with is that the idea of class itself is undermined by that. What we would recognise is that class is a contingent issue. And I have some concerns about what it is the job of the historian is to be. It seems to be fairly straightforward, if you are trying to explain contingent historical events such as wars, revolutions, changes in government, that you have to explain those contingently; but why should we regard history as being about that as opposed to the ordinary mundane lives of men and women? And if you look at that kind of socio-economic level you can say that class has always been a massive predictor of how people do. In a sense, that it is completely obvious.

**KM** You say how they do. How they behave or ...?

**MS** Well things like demographics are very important for explaining people's lives and also for explaining historical dynamics. What worries me about current developments is that we have switched towards political history as being what history is about and we have lost sight of the fact that there are millions of people out there whose lives are very important ....

**EY** I cannot quite buy that. What we are looking at is a larger repertoire of power relations within which people have felt oppressed. So when Richard talks about gender relations, those are ways in which people have experienced their lives and have experienced a sense of powerless or of power: the same is true for race relations and in some situations ethnic relations. These are not only usually relations of so-called difference but relations of inequality and usually depicted by those who have the most power to make definitions in a society, as relations of superiority and inferiority in a moral authority sense. So, I would say that it's not that we are junking class relations but putting a whole bunch of other power relations, within which people live and suffer, on to the historical stage.

**MS** Yes.

**EY** When I think of the industrial revolution, I want to rehabilitate the Hammonds who were sensitive to the sorts of relations in which people lived and how they can be attacked; their great concern was with the unrestrained and unregulated behaviour of people in power, between the period of the French Revolution and around 1845, as being the key force which actually shaped the experience of the industrial revolution rather than just a change in technologies. And that was a kind of change in power relations which not only impacted in a class sense but very much in a gender sense as women and children were dragged into the workforce to break the power of men.

**JS** But women and children had always been in the workforce.

**EY** But they were brought in in a different way, precisely into the public workforce — not at home — in order to be paid lower wages and be redefined as unskilled; in other words to shunt offside male labour which had trade union traditions or which appealed in a customary way to regulative legislation coming out of the Elizabethan period. And this is what is happening now: 'flexibilisation' is synonymous with feminisation because women are always used to break male job control — it doesn't have to be male — and undermine traditions which give working people more control over their work situation. That then ramifies into the traditional authority relations of the family when the women and children can get work and the husband can't. We are living through that again today with the unemployed man feeling very emasculated.

**DP** Listening to you talk about the way in which power relationships are now conceived, it makes it very obvious that we have broadened the whole picture to embrace all sorts of elements which were not there in the more traditional one. But I just wonder, to bring you back to a point that was made earlier when we paused momentarily on the question of the state, whether it has not been at the expense of considering power with a big 'P'. Neither on the Left at the present time in political discourse nor amongst historians is there any great preoccupation with the state in the capital sense. I suppose a traditionalist would argue that surely there is something in the old view that society is structured in a certain way which gives rise to a certain group, class, or élite wielding power in one form or another. And of course the whole notion of a Leviathan state, a powerful state, has been at the heart of many different views of this historical narrative. I wonder whether we are not losing sight of some big questions about power for this very refreshing look at a whole array of power relationships amongst people at another level.

**RE** But you see you are making two assumptions, I think, which some of us would contest. One is that those are the big questions: ultimately political history has the big questions, social and economic history, gender history, ethnic history and so on all have little questions. I think I would want to contest that. Second, there is an assumption in what you say, and possibly in the whole reason why you brought this meeting together, that there is a single agenda amongst historians on the Left. Now this might have been true twenty or thirty years when class seemed a dominant thing and the teleological view that we were all marching towards a glorious socialist future still obtained. But nowadays it is impossible to say there is a single agenda.

**DP** No, I am not arguing that there is a single agenda.

**RE** We have a number of agendas. For some people looking at the micro politics of power at the level of every day life is as important as looking at the commanding heights of the state.

**DP** I'm not making any assumptions, I'm only posing questions. You have rather avoided the question that I was posing. Are we not neglecting an important element of an older tradition in the process of doing these things, which may be enormously valuable; or creating a preferred story or an equally important story?

**RE** But my objection is: who is 'we'? If you say historians, of course it is not true that people are neglecting that. History is such a hugely diverse subject that there are a very large number of historians from various different political and methodological perspectives beavering away precisely at the history of high politics, the state, voting systems, policing and power and control. In some ways the influence of Foucault for example, I think, has directed left-wing historians back towards the repressive apparatus of the state. Look at my own field of modern Germany where the state is impossible to ignore, particularly between 1933 and 1945, there is an enormous amount of work going on. But arguably the traditional history of high politics from a fairly metholodogically and politically conservative point of view — it does not have to be that — that kind of history is still so widely practised that you could describe it as at least in some institutions and areas as being dominant. Progressive or liberal historians, or whatever you like to think of ourselves as, are not necessarily in the majority. We are talking about a specific kind of history here which is betrayed by your use of the term 'we'. I think you haven't quite thought clearly about who you mean when you say 'we'.

**DP** Perfectly true.

**KM** What exactly are you getting at when you talk about the state? Does that imply high politics and almost the Leninist sense of a state you can get hold of. You can also look at the state in the sense of, say, the welfare state and welfare agencies. There is a whole body of literature on the twentieth-century welfare state in its various forms. It doesn't necessarily take the state as its focus and it's not a literature about the state. It's a literature about something else in which the state is an absolutely crucial part. But the state turns out to be something, certainly in twentieth-century society, to be quite variegated and complex and raises lots of different questions of power relations within the state and between, say, welfare or educational providers and the people to whom they providing. To just raise the question of whether we are leaving out the state begs the question of what we mean by the state which is quite a difficult question.

**PJ** We all agree on its importance. But I don't know what David's definition of the state is. Is it the instrument of the possessing classes?

**DP** Oh, certainly not just an instrument. My conception of the state is a sort of Lenin plus Gramsci I suppose, accepting the importance that Gramsci attached to civil society and winning the assent of the population at large for a set of ideas. But I still think that Gramsci's ideas were rooted in a quite traditional and structured view of social relations. Anyway I am not here to expound my own view. Just to put it in very modern terms — a certain amount of damage has been done by the way in which it does not seem to be regarded as so important in political discourse on the Left as to who controls the levers, the commanding heights — and people are finding all sorts of other ways of empowering themselves. Yet, I think, we have a very interesting object lesson with the present government about the importance of controlling these commanding heights; they are still there and they still represent certain interests ...

**MS** My view is that that approach is still very strong but there has been more attention on the way in which the politicians work and try and influence society culturally. If you look at twentieth century history — the work of Ross McKibbin for instance — it's interested in the way in which governing parties such as the Conservative party establish hegemony through cultural means as well as by the pure use of government and institutions alone.[19] So the perspective you outlined is still very pervasive in historiography; but it has broadened out its remit.

**EY** Yes. Class is cultural activity as well as economic position and activity. E.P. Thompson really opened that way of seeing it with *The Making of the English Working Class* because before then the study of the working class was very much confined within a rather classic notion of the Labour Movement with its three wings: the political party — in the British case the Labour Party — the trade Union movement and the cooperative movement. So all preceding events were seen in some way as an onward upward march to this culmination. And of course Thompson broke the mould there by saying that we have to see how people experience their lives and create their collective identities in relation to what they see as other groups and often groups with conflicting interests, over time and through the experience of struggle. And he said that, although we may live in productive relations which very comprehensively constrain our lives, we experience these relations in cultural terms and those are not necessarily predictable nor fixed.

**DP** What you seem to be saying that, if you employ the terms 'class' and 'state' in a cultural sense, these concepts can still be used to help explain power relations; but you feel the old notion of class as a structure or the state as a structure will not do.

**PJ** No I want to separate the state and give it some autonomy, separate it from the possessing classes, for example. I think there is a good post-revisionist argument for saying that the source of the conflict which produces the French Revolution — if you believe it is a product of conflict which I do — is a fight between an unleashed state, which is attacking the possessing classes in the name of modernity. And I wonder whether that did not apply as well in the 1620 and 1630s.

**JS** You could sustain an argument along those lines. The interesting thing which I would stress about England — well there are two things which come readily to mind. One of the peculiarities of English history in the sixteenth and seventeenth centuries was that the state however defined was very weak, compared to say Habsburg Spain in the sixteenth century or France in the seventeenth and, if we are looking at the peculiar trajectories of English commercial development in the seventeenth century, I do think that the lack of the state as an extractive element is something which is crucial to English economic development. Another peculiarity of the English social system in the seventeenth century was the way in which the interface between state and society was really a very close one. It depends on how you define the state of course but central government was dependent on having its affairs run on a county level by the cooperation of amateur office-holders, gentry and nobility who were operating as JPs, sheriffs, and so on. It was also dependent at a parish level which is where, I think, one can connect some of the more familiar grand narratives with the sort of concerns expressed by Richard. There has been an enormous amount of work done on relationships at a community level in early modern England and other early modern states and one of the points about the state in a society like early modern England is that it is dependent on the presence of what is in effect a fifth column within every village to try and implement state policies.[20] If you look at an English village in any part of the seventeenth century the secular law is implemented by Parish constables who are unpaid amateurs usually drawn from the upper ranks of the peasantry. So immediately you have got a local power structure being invoked in what goes on. Church affairs are being implemented by a combination of vicars and churchwardens, the latter again drawn from the upper stratum of the peasantry. You do not, of course, have a welfare state in the seventeenth century but by the standards of the time quite an effective and ambitious poor law system, administrated locally by overseers of the poor who are again drawn from upper people in the village. So there is a problem of sorting out the state from society. The state or central authority does seem to depend on local people, often within village communities. And the fact those people are often or normally chosen from the upper stratum of village society — the upper stratum of male village society of course — does mean that you have a connection between the affairs of central government if you like and local power structures and local power conflicts with the village. Ultimately, although, I am nervous of a definition of the state which sees it purely in terms of the possessing classes — bureaucracies evolve their own being — I think it is a matter of some interest that the English state, before say the nineteenth century, depends on people of property including people of fairly small property to run its business in the localities.

## Historical objectivity and political relativism

DP We should move on. Richard, a couple of moments ago, you made the suggestion that what I was trying to defend was a Left view of history. That is quite interesting because some of the critics of your own book said that you were actually in that book defending a Leftish view against a conservative one. Eileen, in conversation before we came here, asked me if I thought that there was a revisionism of the Left particularly in terms of attitudes towards class and gender and developing, a sense of different identities and identity politics and so on. I just wanted to ask whether you thought the description of this dialogue which has gone on is correctly encapsulated in a notion of defending a Leftish view of history against a conservative revisionism or whether it is more complex than that and whether there is a Left revisionism.

**RE** Well it is more complex of course. I think in writing my book I tried to steer a course between conservative defenders of a view that 'all you have to do in history is to be completely neutral and objective and read the documents and hey presto here is the truth and it doesn't have any political relevance at all' on the one hand, and radical postmodernist sceptics on the other hand who say 'historians make it all up, we just read into the documents whatever we like and we produce, indeed should produce, whatever is useful to our own political purposes'. So of course I was fallen upon by both sides; though more by the conservatives because they have more influence in the daily papers. So far there are very few postmodernists who review for the *Sunday Telegraph* — probably because the readers would not appreciate the style they write in. I was not defending a specifically Left view of history against conservatives. It seems to me that I was defending a broad, catholic diverse conception of history against a narrow view; the view put by many conservative historians that really the history of high politics is what is the core of history.

There is of course a Left view of that, and that is what I suspected at points you were representing yourself — what you described as the traditional story that's been put around by Left wing historians of the march of progress through the English and French revolutions and the labour movement up to the present day. That seems to me, too, to be a narrow conception of history. On the Left and more generally as well there is now quite rightly an enormous diversity of ways of approaching and understanding and researching and writing and teaching history. That's all to the good. Modern society is so complex that different people ask very, very different questions of history and it is not realistic to think that we can go back to any kind of common denominators. Even in writing textbooks on modern European history, let us say, it is not obvious to me that those textbooks should give space to the French Revolution or industrialisation as major motors of change. There are many different ways in which general surveys can be written.

That having been said, what does worry me, and one thing we have not discussed yet, is that on some parts of the Left there is a view that history has nothing at all to do with objectivity or with facts; that it is only useful politically if people write history in such a way that it is politically useful. This sounds awfully circular in the way that I have put it. But let us say that if you wish to write history for a political purpose, you just plunder history for whatever you need for your own politics and you put it all together so that it supports your present-day point of view. It seems to me that is very dangerous. I don't think most historians actually do that.

I think most historians have the 'still small voice' at the back of their mind which says: when we come to the documents and we would like the documents to support some point of view and they don't that still small voice says 'oh dear, watch out, you have to throw your favourite views out of the window, they've just got no support in the material you are looking at'. If we, as it were, disregard that still small voice, or say it's not important, or go at history simply in order to collect examples and materials to support our own present-day point of view, then that is dangerous; and it's dangerous because, contrary to the assumption of a number of people who have put this point of view — what we might call the postmodernists — it's not necessarily left-wing at all; it can just as well be right-wing. You can say: right, well, I'm a neo-fascist, I'll just plunder the past to support my own neo-fascist point of view. And if you believe that all points of view are equally valid, that all historians ever do is that, you have no means of countering that argument at all. The only way you can actually distinguish between versions of history and nail the lies of latent neo-fascism, if you want to put it brutally, is to have some general notion of objectivity. Not in terms of some hard-and-fast-for-all-time truth that you discover and is never going to be changed, but objectivity in the sense of what the records left to us allow us to say and what they do not allow us to say. And they allow us to say many things and they allow us to argue with each other. But you reach some kind of boundary and you step beyond that if you plunder the past for your own political purposes.

**DP** I am interested to know who these people are on the Left to whom you refer and why you think they are falling into this sort of mode of thinking. As you say, it is very dangerous and could open up a space for people on the extreme right.

**RE** Well this kind of approach is more common in writing about history than in actually writing history. It's much easier to find people who say that this is how history ought to be written than to find examples of it. For the obvious reason that examples of it will tend to get stamped on by historians fairly quickly. But, I think, the answer is that for people on the Left the question often is how we can make history political useful.

There used to be the idea, twenty or thirty years ago, that Marxist history was scientific it uncovered the laws of motion of human society and these laws showed objectively that the working class would win there would be a revolution and the future that Marxists desired would come about. So there was a very neat dovetailing of a belief in scientific history and the purposes of the labour movement, socialism, communism or whatever. That has now been exploded so that — with the fall of Marxism and the decline of class as a central factor in postmodern societies — if you are going to make history politically useful it's very difficult to reconcile that notion with some kind of objective history because it might not be politically convenient. One way of saying what I am trying to do in my book is to resurrect the notion that it is actually possible to be a serious historian, observing a notion of objectivity and yet write history that is politically committed and politically relevant. But I am afraid that there is a fairly widespread view among postmodernists, who think of themselves as radical and progressive, that that is not possible.

**DP** The problem of relativism bothered me increasingly as I thought about this discussion because nobody was more committed in the period after the war to writing a history of the English Revolution which was relevant to the struggles in the post-war period and which put struggle 'from below' right at the forefront of their considerations, than the group of historians in the Communist Party. And yet they wrote a history which was defensible as history in its own terms at that time.

**KM** Well you could say that Christopher Hill and others at that time also wrote things which were quite indefensible about the Russian Revolution. There were also signs of the danger of that approach.

**RE** Christopher Hill did after all write a book called *Lenin and the Russian Revolution*. [21]

**KM** If you plough back through the old *Modern Quarterly* there are one or two pieces ....

**DP** Do you put this down to the fact that he strayed out of what he really knew and therefore became a less good historian or simply do you put it down to a teleology?

**KM** I think there was a political commitment which overrode the sort of critical objections which could have been made by any specialist in the field. The commitment overrode that sort of objectivity. A similar reason would have been given I'm sure — as with the postmodernists — that you cannot obtain objectivity. It was a Marxist version of the idea that everybody is positioned; that is where I am positioned therefore that is what I write. If you look at something like James Klugman's history of the British Communist Party, writing at as a functionary of the CP, that is what exactly what he says at the beginning. Everybody takes sides.[22] This is the side I have taken. So therefore if you find something conveniently omitted, basically that's the explanation. It is not all that far away from what you are saying about various postmodernist histories.

**DP** But it's bad history isn't it? You could also point to the great development of history 'from below' which enlarged our field of study. The work that Georges Rudé did was very much within an old-fashioned structural framework but certainly it was good history in the sense that it enlarged our knowledge of what was happening and what was happening to real people.

**PJ** If it was good history then why has it run into the sand now? Why has social history of this type just run out of steam?. I think social history was one of the questions you were asking us to discuss. Social history in my view ran out of steam because it perhaps has been too focused and has been replaced by cultural history which has a wider remit.

**RE** Well it's run out of steam as away of explaining other things like political history but it has not run out of steam in itself. If you look around the world of history and historians there are very large numbers of people writing social history.

**PJ** The kind of social history that David is describing — of the lower orders?

## Broadening Marxism

**JS** I'd like to return to a number of points that Eileen raised a little while ago. One of the things that has happened to all periods from the medieval period through to the twentieth century has been a tremendous broadening of the subject matter of social history. I have problems with the concept of cultural history — I just don't understand what it is because nobody has ever come up with a suitable explanation unless you work out from an anthropological idea of culture. Quite where social history stops and cultural history begins is a problem. But, if one can expect the use of social history to include things like *mentalités*, I think there has been a tremendous broadening in the subject area of social history over the past twenty years as we are all aware. This has implications for the type of grand narrative that perhaps Rudé was interested in. I think one of the reasons why Marxism in particular has had so little impact on my generation of social historians working on early modern England is that it doesn't seem — and perhaps we are being rather short sighted — to answer a lot of the questions in which we are becoming increasingly interested. Quite how Marxism bears on a witchcraft accusation I would be very uncertain, for example. One of the consequences of this broadening of the subject matter has been to fragment knowledge, which is another problem for us all. We are entering areas like ritual, like popular religion, even some aspects of crime and law enforcement where certainly a traditionalist might have difficulty. Thompson, before his death, was producing some very interesting reformulations about how Marxism might be used to open up these areas but a lot of these areas being developed by social historians do take them away from the accepted grand narratives and also away from contact with Marxist theory.

**EY** Well I am not sure. One of the things which I hang on to from Marxism which seems to me infinitely transposable is the idea of dialectical materialism. You are always looking for contradictions, conflicts, dissonances, which might actually be the source of movement as they are negotiated. Now where these dissonances are going to appear in any social formation is partly a matter of empirical identification. No single model of conflict is sacrosanct. You build whatever your model is, then you engage with more material and you keep modifying your theory. Some of the cultural Marxists — if you want to bring Raymond Williams in and certainly E.P. Thompson — never kept their exploration of tensions and conflicts only at a public workplace level. They were into all sorts of customs and religious recreational and educational practices; culture itself was a theatre of contention or possible tension.[23] So I do not agree that there is something unusable about Marxism which is not suited to the kinds of areas that you find interesting now.

**KM** Would you think that, by the time of his later work, Thompson was a Marxist in a different sense?

**EY** Sure.

**KM** In a sense Marxism itself had become a lot more diffuse. If you think of Thompson's book on Blake, which he wrote just before he died, its not what you have recognised as a Marxist work thirty years earlier when you are talking about the heyday of this type of history.

**EY** But there is a long tradition of cultural Marxism going back to people like Volosinov who really looked at language — which is supposed to be the postmodernists' property — language as a form of social communication and contestable at that. Social classes battle over the same signs which they invest with different meanings; it is the fact that certain signs — like 'the people' or other bits of rhetoric — carry diverse meanings which makes them so dynamic and so endlessly attractive. There are traditions within Marxism which have run down these paths.[24] Although, I agree, Thompson did not start by addressing these issues he ended up by regarding even the notion of 'custom' as area of contention; because everyone in the early eighteenth century if they wanted to be persuasive had to say what they were arguing had the authority of custom behind it: something that happened last week could be called a customary practice.

**MS** Can I go back to this question about the history of the Left which obviously bears on the question of Marxism? I think we agreed earlier that the whole historicist explanation was now discredited. And, of course, there are problems there because the terms we use including things like 'Left' and 'Right' do have their own history and a kind of historicist heritage. So there is a real issue about how do we think of the Left in ways which don't fall into the trap which we have exposed. I think Marxism continues to be an important critical tool and I am struck that — despite the collapse of the Marxist project particularly in Eastern Europe — how Marxism as an intellectual tool has not faded away. It's still a live issue; we are still talking about it here ten years after the end of Marxism's demise as a project. Yet, given that we reject the historicist roots of Marxism, what does this lead on to? Does it lead to a reclaiming of lost potentials in the past rather than a notion of a kind of ongoing political project? The question of what actually is a coherent Marxism is still one to which we have not got an obvious answer at this stage.

**RE** Well Marxism has, I think, run into intellectual problems as well as political problems. If I think of my own field of modern German history when I started in the early 1970s — we all seem to be reminiscing about the good old days when we started and things were much more simple than they are now — Marxist explanations were dominant. People were thinking of why did Hitler come to power, why did Nazism happen, how do you explain the Third Reich? One broad explanation was that the German bourgeoisie had failed to conquer power in 1848 as the bourgeoisie had done in the English and French Revolutions. The German revolution failed and the aristocracy were then able to carry on running society and preventing any liberal or democratic state and society from emerging. Now that has been completely exploded in the last ten or fifteen years. It is quite clear now that German society was much more mobile and much more dynamic than anybody had previously thought and what might be broadly described as bourgeois values absolutely permeated German society by 1914. So, if you cannot explain it by a deficit of bourgeois values or a failure of the bourgeoisie to gain social and political hegemony, then that whole class and Marxist way of trying to explain the disasters in the first half of this century in Germany really collapses.

There is another respect — even more serious I think — in which Marxism ran into huge difficulties in German history. When I started, a lot of people tended to see Nazi Germany and the Third Reich in class terms and a lot of work went on trying to show how Nazism was in some the sense the vehicle of certain social classes: the petty bourgeoisie, then joined by the broad middle class, with a large input of big business, and so on. Those were the terms in which people tried to write about Nazism. But in recent years our understanding of Nazism has shifted very strongly towards putting race at the centre. Not just the Nazi anti-Semitism but the whole way in which the Nazis stigmatised, sterilised and indeed murdered other minorities, whether it be homosexuals or gypsies or the handicapped with nearly 200,00 of whom, handicapped Germans, were deliberately exterminated by the Nazis — and then in a broader sense during the war Poles, and particularly Russians — nearly 4 million Russian POWs deliberately killed by the Nazis. It has become clear that the centre of the Nazi world view was race and racism in a very comprehensive, thoroughgoing sense and, disturbingly, that this had a certain appeal to a considerable sector of the German working class. Ironically, the more you have detailed local studies of everyday life under Nazism, studies of perpetrators of one sort or another and studies of victims, the more difficult it has become to sustain that simple class way of understanding the Third Reich.

Other aspects of that interpretation have really fallen victim to empirical research as well, particularly the role of big business in bringing Nazism to power — although not its role during the Third Reich once it had come to power. I don't know how far this is connected with broader political problems that Marxism has had but intellectually it has reached the end of its explanatory usefulness in some key areas.

**KM** Is there not a distinction between a heroic model of class in the sense which you are saying is unsustainable and class as a tool of analysis. A tool of analysis can either be not very much use at all or it can be very useful in terms of particular social relations, forms of behaviour or political allegiance. In terms of British society you can think in terms of working class racism and you can think in terms of working class conservatism. You obviously cannot explain these things simply by class but it's a key tool of analysis and not one we can set aside very easily.

**RE** Sure. Take the whole business of voting. Who were the 13 million people who voted for the Nazis in 1932? It used to be done in class terms. Now there have been some very sophisticated statistical analyses which have shown that in fact the Nazis had a very broad appeal to all social classes — not quite equal — but they got a very substantial number of working-class votes. And that does then open up the question of what they were appealing to in the working class that made the working class join in with all the others. That alters our understanding without entirely throwing the concept out of the window; but as a simple, one-way explanation it has gone now.

**MS** I think we need to be careful though to recognise that Marxism isn't necessarily focused on class. Another main topic is capitalism. You might construct an explanation of German fascism, which I know little about, in terms of ideas of race and purity appealing in a complex depressed capitalist economy. It would not be a determinist appeal but it would still be one which would have some links to a Marxist notion of a dynamic capitalist economy.

**DP** It seems to me that Marxism was not just about a political project except that many people made it essentially about that. It was a critique of capitalism. And if you want a very simple answer as to why we are still talking about it, still remains useful. As long as capitalism exists Marxism is going to tell us something about how it operates; maybe not everything and maybe we have to be much more cautious than we were and we have to take in all the points that people have made about the way we handle class and the concept of the state but Marxism still tells you something about how capitalism operates and in whose interests it operates.

**RE** It was a political project. Come on!

**EY** But Marxism isn't ossified. I do think that feminists have opened up all kinds of questions which Marxists haven't necessarily answered and which challenge certain classical Marxist notions in a very fundamental way: notions of work and production, which presume that the kind of people involved in the process are making goods or services for sale in the market. A lot of human beings, especially women, expend a lot of energy on useful tasks which never get in any way into the market place. Skill is an issue. When women do jobs they are called unskilled; when men do the same jobs, particularly if they have trade union clout, the jobs became skilled. You can see very interesting empirical examples of this. Women spun at home in the domestic economy; that was unskilled work. Then, when spinning moved into the factory and at the point when men got hold of it and their trade unions became reasonably powerful suddenly, it was a wonderfully skilled occupation and weaving went the opposite way.

**MS** I think a big intellectual problem with Marxism is the Labour theory of value which was the core and it was a way of linking a theory of capitalism to a theory of class. It is now difficult to defend for the kind of reasons you were saying, Eileen: where does work stop and non-work begin and how do you distinguish exploiters from exploited? As far as I know there is no Marxist economist left who would really be happy with using that concept. And that does open up the question of — well Marxism continues to inspirational — but as a cohesive body of thought what is left of it really? You can have a theory of capitalism which does not involve a theory of class perhaps.

## Social and socialist history

**KM** If you think of Marxism as a critique of capitalism and also as a political project there is still a lot that it does not address. Think of the history of the Soviet Union. It is actually quite difficult, just using class in any crude way too see how Marxism might be applied to the social history of the Soviet Union. That is, incidentally, why I would think there is a actually a very great deal of mileage left in social history, because if you take the Soviet Union the possibilities of social history are only just opening up. It hadn't really started in the 1980s and certainly not with the sort of materials with which you can actually interrogate in more complex ways what went on in Stalin's Russia.

**PJ** In what sense do we perceive social history to be in crisis then? As we clearly do.

**DP** Well you did and a number of people said 'hold on'.

**JS** I think I said two three times that it was doing very nicely.

**RE** It is in a crisis, I think, in two respects though I would not accept that it is disappearing, outmoded or has vanished. The first is that it did have in the 1970s and the early 1980s this hegemonic claim. You find people saying things like social history is history, all history is social history because all history has a social dimensions. A very big claim: and, I think, that is gone. There were a large number of historians who never accepted that in the first place, but the number has now got larger. That's connected with the second reason why it is in crisis, which is that a large number of the youngest generation of historians — PhD. students and young professional historians — are not doing social history anymore; they are doing cultural history.

**PJ** I would endorse that. I think that in the French case the contamination of social history with socialist history was what, at a given moment, started to put people off; the feeling that it could only be studied according to a given agenda of topics, and the way those topics were studied was very mechanistic. Social identities were derived from economic function, or rhetoric analysed in terms of economic position. A whole bunch of American historians, in particular, simply decided to stay clear of what they called the quagmires of social history, and they moved out into cultural history, entirely properly because they wished to cut adrift from this imbroglio of constant social, socialist reinterpretation of the French Revolution, its causes and so on.

**DP** But it was a socialist interpretation not just a social one, that's what you are saying?

**PJ** Well, very largely it was. That is what alienated them from it.

**DP** Because I have very great difficulty in distinguishing between what you are describing as social history and cultural history.

**PJ** Well a wider agenda. You are not solely preoccupied by Chartism for example, by working class formation. When I came to the University of Birmingham the only form of social history done was the study of Chartism under the inspiration of Dorothy Thompson. That just ran into the sand as an interesting topic of study. It couldn't navigate its way out, as it were, so it died. Dorothy retired and it died. Social history was only reborn relatively recently for our students when they discovered that social history could also be the history of consumerism or the social history of the Tory party.

**EY** I would not actually have thought of social history as represented only by the history of Chartism. I thought it was also the sort of stuff that Brian Harrison was doing in the early days in *Drink and the Victorians*,[25] taking all kinds of everyday activities and showing how complicated their politics were. Class was very much at the centre of that thinking — not necessarily a Marxist view of class — but class groups in relation to each other. I am not sure how you are defining cultural history or seeing it. I guess I consider myself a practitioner.

**PJ** Well Jim mentioned *mentalités*. That was an improvement on the old social history project as far as I'm concerned, and one from a quite different tradition — from *Annales* history.

**JS** In the early reviews of my big social history textbook[26] one of the reviewers said that about a third of the book is devoted to subjects not normally considered to be within the social historian's remit and that was the third of the book that was trying to deal with what the French would call *mentalités*. I take very much your point about what would now seem a very old fashioned subject like Chartism. But I do have problems about defining exactly what cultural history is and I do think that, if you accept that the social historian is concerned with culture or with *mentalités*, then an awful lot of cultural history is subsumed into what social historians do.

**PJ** I agree. I am just saying that social history needed replenishing at a particular moment when it had run out of approved topics.

**RE** I think we should rehabilitate this distinction a bit. I do think there is a difference to be made. Social history, particularly in the 1970s and early 1980s, was into quantification for example, all those grand quantitative analyses of different social classes in different cities or parts of cities — Geoff Crossick's work on Deptford or Stephan Thernstrom's *The Other Bostonians* — all that kind of thing, looking at social structure, looking at social relations, classes, groups of one sort or another.[27] I do think that at that time very few people were really writing or researching about what you might call *mentalités* or attitudes or culture in that sense. You can't imagine anyone now in 1998 actually starting a research project which is going to be the quantitative analysis of the social structure of Birmingham. If they are going to do Birmingham, they are going to look at clubs, societies and their relationship to culture — that sort of thing.

**PJ** Sociability.

**RE** That's the change that has happened.

**KM** Actually what has happened to cultural history or to traditional art history is the writing of social history into it.

**EY** Absolutely right.

**KM** If you look at *A History of Art* when they reprint a volume from thirty years ago they will have to bung in a new introduction and basically what the introduction will be about is the social dimension of things which once would have been seen simply in aesthetic terms.

**RE** Art historians are catching up with history as it was written twenty years ago. It's not what we mean by social history.

## Postmodernism again

**DP** In the midst of all the considerations we have been looking at postmodernism has entered into the discussion at one or two moments. It was interesting in the dialogue with you all before we came here, that there were contrary views about how much it impinges on these issues and whether it is really part of the 'crisis' we are facing in social history or whether we can basically keep paddling the canoe in the direction we are pointing.

**PJ** Well, I think, I put the cat among the pigeons, David, by saying I did not know what postmodernism is; you instructed me manfully, sent me a photocopy which increased my understanding,[28] and by that time I had read Richard's book so I had a clearer notion. If you can sum it up in that remark by Hayden White that 'historians produce verbal fiction the contents of which are as much invented as formed' — then I don't agree. And if I felt that postmodernism has had any impact on what I do as basically a rural historian, I suppose, or any impact on how I do it, then I would probably resent that remark as well. But my position is one of indifference in the meantime.

**DP** And yet you are attracted to cultural history and some of these impetuses have come — or have they not come — I am unsure about this — out of the postmodern stable?

**PJ** That begs the question of what it is. I started off by thinking that it is nothing to do with language and that it is nothing to do with gender; now if are you are subsuming gender and linguistic analysis then I begin to understand it a little better than I did.

**EY** I think there is a history of concern with language and gender which is quite separate from postmodernism which then maybe overlaps or converges with it in certain places, though not all; if you can remember yourself back to the 1960s and 1970s when E.P. Thompson liberated the study of class for some of us so that we could study religion as well as the workplace and think about class conflicts in cultural fields; when community, people's and oral history were another impulse which was insisting that the voice from so-called 'below' be included in the public record and historical story; when the women's liberation movement especially was very vigorous in rethinking historical narrative and putting a great emphasis on language as being a restricting or liberating business; and of course when there were black liberation movements all over the world too. Now, I notice that in the definition of postmodernism which you kindly gave to us feminist history is featured as a big area of postmodernism. Well I refuse that. To me it comes out of the women's movement to begin with and the questions which were posed have real vibrancy still in terms of political needs and projects, although obviously we want to be analytically scrupulous. I'm just not going to float around in an area which says that historians only make meaning through their language, full stop. If postmodernism has accentuated these developments, which were already coming from elsewhere as part of political movements or projects, then well and good.

There are things which I find very valuable which come out of this political moment in the 1960s and 1970s and which postmodernism may have echoed. I do like the emphasis on constructions of identity within real lived power relations of class, gender, race which have deeply affected people's life chances. And I do like the emphasis on discourse — knowledge which has power in a certain cultural formation; and also on language, particularly rhetoric, which is the language of persuasion. It is valuable, too, to think about the way in which people construct their own identities especially in reaction to identities imposed on them by other groups of people. The kind of history I now write is the history of a cultural moment in which there are different groups of people interacting, except I will privilege representation, discourse, rhetoric; so I have taken something from somewhere — maybe from postmodernism — but I don't really live within that label.[29]

**JS** I have not gone as far into to those subject areas as you have Eileen but I have brushed up against community power structures, gender, and things like that without any conscious reference to postmodernism. We do live in a postmodern world — Keith Jenkins assures of that[30] — and the basis of our discussion is the fact that, despite two thirds of the population saying they are working class, I find it increasingly difficult to look at present day society in terms of classic class structure.

The biggest *problem* I have with postmodernism is the rejection of the idea of objectivity, of truth. Now I accept this a big issue which we are not going to resolve in five minutes. But I should just like to give you two ranging shots. One is an article which unfortunately I haven't had a chance to read by Alan Sokal called 'Transgressing the Boundaries Towards a Transformative Hermeneutics of Quantum Gravity' published in *Social Texts* 1996 whereby a practising physicist submitted an article to a postmodernist literary journal, demonstrating that gravity was a rhetorical device. This was accepted and published.[31] The point being that, with the lines of logic which postmodernism encourages, it is very difficult to prove whether or not an argument is fallacious. Reading this I was reminded of Winston Smith, in the closing pages of Orwell's *1984*, sitting at the table in the Chestnut Tree café, writing 'two plus two equals ...' and being unable to find the number to go there. He recalls that his interrogator, O'Brien, claimed that he could float off the floor like a soap bubble. Winston concludes that if O'Brien thinks that and that he, Winston, simultaneously thinks he saw it then 'the thing happens'. There follows this passage:

Suddenly, like a lump of submerged wreckage breaking the surface of water, the thought burst into his [i.e. Winston Smith's] mind: 'It doesn't really happen. We imagine it. It is hallucination'. He pushed the thought under instantly. The fallacy was obvious. It presupposed that somewhere or other, outside oneself, there was a 'real' world where 'real' things happened. But how could there be such a world? What knowledge do we have anything, save through our own minds? All happenings are in the mind. Whatever happens in all minds, truly happens.[32]

Now post-Enlightenment objectivity might have its problems as an intellectual system and the search for truth might be a problematic one but I do think it rather beats that.

**RE** Eileen described postmodernism as a label, and I think that is right. We are not talking about an organised body of ideas, least of all a lot of people who all agree with each other. But it is a kind of convenient label. And like all these labels, different people understand them in different ways. Marxism might be just as good an example of a label.

You can use postmodernism in a rather narrow sense, if you want, about certain kinds of theoretical approaches and the influence of certain writers and philosophers. Foucault comes to mind for example. He's had a substantial influence on historians — a man who did not describe himself as postmodernist — but nevertheless whose influence one can describe as being postmodernist. You can use it in terms of specific writings about history where it has been most commonly used by self-confessed postmodernists who wish to challenge history as a form of cognition or knowledge about the past which is based on an ability to recover certain real things about the past.

Or you can use it in a much broader sense — and I still think it's rather useful to do that — to describe a general reorientation of thought that has happened in a patchy and uneven way over the last twenty years maybe, perhaps even longer in some areas, and which has become particularly noticeable in the 1990s. That is precisely what we have been talking about — in other ways a move of thought away from modern culture and thought, which is based on notions of progress in quite a linear sort of way and notions of scientific objectivity, towards a very different set of ideas; and particularly in terms of history away from social and economic determination towards cultural and linguistic determination. If you take feminist history, the change in feminist history from looking at the history of women to the history of gender or the concepts of language by which masculinity and femininity are defined, I would say that it useful to describe that as part of postmodernist orientation.

**DP** But it did seem to me that in your book you stretched your definition when you included, by implication at least, books like Natalie Zemon Davis's book on Martin Guerre, which I had always put in an *Annales/mentalités* school of thought.[33]

**RE** Yes — it's interesting because there are obviously some books and some approaches which you can fit into a number of different ways of looking at things. But it seems to me undeniably true that among historians there has been a move away from big theories, big models, big explanations and indeed even big topics of the sort we were used to in the seventies, towards much smaller kinds of objects and more restricted methods. This has pluses and minuses, but there is a way in which historians have looked much more to small communities and humble individuals and that has become more common in the nineties. And you can look at books like *The Return of Martin Guerre,* which, has been a model for many historians who have moved in that direction and, raises certain very important questions about the way historians treat the past, because Davis confesses in the preface that 'what I offer you in part is my own invention'. That seems to me in a away to encapsulate what nobody including the author at the time might have thought of as a postmodern way of looking at history but certainly does now.

**KM** Postmodernism in that very broad sense does bring in a lot of people who would not necessarily think of themselves as postmodernists and a lot of what it involves was already prefigured in the 1960s and 1970s; Patrick Joyce says that historians should welcome postmodernism because, given their relativism and scepticism, there would seem to be some common ground. I would agree that scepticism, relativism, contingency, the concern with the particular are things which would actually distinguish history from some of the other social sciences. A mild variety of postmodernism does not cause me any problem at all. The sticking point really comes with Jim's point about objectivity, about truth and also about empathy: the idea that we can't reach a degree of perfect empathy or perfect truth, therefore we don't go for as much as of the partial empathy or the partial truth as we can get through rational methods of enquiry. That, it seems to me, is the element in some post-modernism which is incompatible with serious historical scholarship.

**MS** I just think we need to distinguish postmodernism as a critique which is in a way where it comes from — as a critique of enlightenment thought. It seems to me that our conversation here is entirely postmodern; what we are saying is that the great narratives: the French Revolution, the English Revolution, the industrial revolution are now all problematic and everything is very complex. I agree with Kevin that we are all postmodernists now; we live in a world of intellectual uncertainty. Then there is postmodernism in a narrow sense which has almost tried to become a school in its own right. This is contradictory, as you can't create a school when you are also saying that the idea of having distinct schools is no longer tenable. In labour history and class, whilst Patrick Joyce is influential and interesting, his attempt to construct postmodernism as having the answers to labour history's problems is ultimately unconvincing.[34]

**DP** I am not too sure on what note to conclude. It seems that postmodernism is useful or not depending on what you think it is and this is undoubtedly a debate which is going to go on and on. But I thought the last part of the conversation was very positive in one sense; it showed — at least to us — that History both as a discipline and a subject and including social history is very much alive and that it is amenable to our investigations. We leave it to our readers to judge how much remains — should remain — of the grand narrative and of Leftist and Marxist historical concepts.

## Notes

1. R.J. Evans, *In Defence of History* (London, 1997).
2. R.H. Tawney, 'The Rise of the Gentry 1558–1640', *Economic History Review* 9 (1941), pp.1–38.
3. That is, the University of Leeds.
4. See G. Lefèbvre, *Les paysans du Nord pendant la Révolution française* (Bari 1959); 'La Révolution française et les paysans' in *Etudes sur la Révolution française* (Paris, 1954).
5. A. Soboul, *Les sans culottes parisiens en l'an II* (Paris, 1958).
6. See D. Guérin, *Class Struggle in the First French Republic: Bourgeois and Bras-Nus, 1793-an II* (London, 1977); A. Ado, *Paysans en Révolution: terre, pouvoir et jacquerie 1789–1794* (Paris, 1996).
7. G.V. Taylor, 'Non-capitalist Wealth and the Origins of the French Revolution', *American Historical Review*, 72 (1967) p.491.
8. J.C.D. Clark, *English Society 1688–1832: Ideology, social structures and political practice during the Ancien Régime* (Cambridge, 1985); *Revolution and Rebellion: State and society in England in the seventeenth and eighteenth centuries* (Cambridge, 1986).
9. J. Smail, *The Origins of Middle Class Culture: Halifax, Yorkshire 1660–1780* (Ithaca, 1994).

10. N. Smelser, *Social Change and the Industrial Revolution* (London, 1959); T. Parsons, *The Social System* (Glencoe, Illinois, 1951); E.P. Thompson, *The Making of the English Working Class* (London, 1963).
11. R. Brenner (1976), 'Agrarian class structure and economic development in pre-industrial Europe', *Past and Present* (1976), pp.29–75, and the ensuing debate in 1978 and 1979, subsequently printed as *The Brenner Debate*, T.H. Aston and C.H.E. Philpin (eds) (Cambridge, 1985).
12. D. Cannadine (1980) *Lords and Landlords: The aristocracy and the towns, 1774–1967* (Leicester, 1980); W.D. Rubinstein, *Wealth and Inequality in Britain* (London, 1986).
13. See E. Hobsbawm, *Labouring Men: Studies in the history of Labour* (London 1964) chs 5 and 7; R.M. Hartwell 'Interpretations of the Industrial Revolution in England', *Journal of Economic History*, 19 (1959), and his 'The Rising Standard of Living in England 1800–50', *Economic History Review*, 13 (1961); Sir J. Clapham, *An Economic History of Modern Britain: The railway age, 1820–1850*, vol.1 (Cambridge, 1926); J.L. Hammond, 'The Industrial Revolution and Discontent', *Economic History Review*, 2 (1930).
14. See K. Baker (ed.), *The French Revolution and the Creation of Modern Political Culture*, vol.1: *The Political Culture of the Old Regime* (Oxford, 1987).
15. E.A. Wrigley, 'The Process of Modernization and the Industrial Revolution in England', *Journal of Interdisciplinary History*, 3 (1972) pp.225–59, reprinted in E.A. Wrigley, *People Cities and Wealth: The triumph of traditional society* (Oxford, 1987), pp.46–74.
16. François Furet, *Penser la Révolution française* (Paris, 1978); *Le passé d'une illusion* (Paris, 1995).
17. D. Blackbourn and G. Eley, *The Peculiarities of German History* (Oxford, 1984).
18. See C.G. Moses, *French Feminism in the Nineteenth Century* (Albany, New York, 1984) pp.9–15; J. Landes, *Women and the Public Sphere in the Age of the French Revolution* (Ithaca 1988); Joan W. Scott, *Only Paradoxes to Offer: French feminists and the Rights of Man* (Cambridge, MA, 1966) ch.2; E.J. Yeo, *Radical Femininity: Women's self-representation in the public sphere* (Manchester, 1998).
19. R. McKibbin, *The Ideologies of Class* (Oxford, 1990).
20. See P. Griffiths, A. Fox and S. Hindle, *The Experience of Authority in Early Modern England* (London, 1996).
21. C. Hill, *Lenin and the Russian Revolution* (London, 1947).
22. J. Klugman, *History of the Communist Party of Great Britain: Formation and early years* (London, 1968), p.11.
23. R. Williams, *The Long Revolution 1960* (London, 1961) Part 2, and *Marxism and Literature* (Oxford, 1977); E.P. Thompson, *Customs in Common* (Penguin, Harmondsworth, 1991).
24. V.N. Volosinov, *Marxism and the Philosophy of Language*, trans L. Matejka and I. Titunik (Cambridge, MA, 1929); F. Jameson, *The Political Unconscious: Narrative as a socially symbolic act* (Ithaca, 1981); J. Epstein, *Radical Expression: Political language, Ritual and Symbol in England 1790–1850* (New York, 1994); see also F.

Jameson, *Jameson on Postmodernism* (London, 1997).
25. B. Harrison, *Drink and the Victorians: the Temperance Question in England, 1815–1872* (London, 1971); see also, E. and S. Yeo, *Popular Culture and Class Conflict 1590–1914* (Brighton, 1981).
26. J. Sharpe, *Early Modern England: A social history 1550–1760* (London, 1977).
27. G. Crosswick, *The Lower Middle Class in Britain 1870–1914* (London, 1977); S. Thernstrom, *The Other Bostonians: Property and progress in the American metropolis, 1880–1970* (Cambridge, MA, 1973).
28. M. Bentley. 'Approaches to Modernity: Western historiography since the Enlightenment' in *The Routledge Companion to Historiography* (London, 1997) M. Bentley (ed.), pp.489–90.
29. See E. Yeo, *The Contest for Social Science: Relations and representations of gender and class* (London, 1996).
30. Keith Jenkins, *Re-Thinking History* (London and New York, 1991).
31. This article is reproduced in A. Sokal and J. Bricmont, *Intellectual Impostures: Postmodern philosophers' abuse of science* (London, 1998).
32. George Orwell, *1984* (Penguin, Harmondsworth, 1954), p.240.
33. N.Z. Davis, *The Return of Martin Guerre* (Cambridge, MA, 1981).
34. P. Joyce, *Visions of the People* (Cambridge, 1990).

# The English Revolution
The decline and fall of revisionism

*Brian Manning*

---

'Revisionism', has been since the late 1970s the orthodox interpretation of English history in the first half of the seventeenth century, and still shapes teaching in universities and schools. The revisionist historians themselves accept the label, which became the common historical parlance. But revisionism never occupied the entire field of historical study. It focused on politics and the ruling class, but during the period of its dominance there also developed and flourished the study of popular culture and popular movements — 'history from below' — and the discovery was made that the nobility and gentry were not the only inhabitants of England, and that as well as men there were also women and children. Examples of this trend are collections of essays such as Barry Reay (ed.) *Popular Culture in Seventeenth-Century England* (1985), Frederick Krantz (ed.) *History from Below: Studies in popular protest and popular ideology* (1988), and Tim Harris (ed.) *Popular Culture in England c.1500–1850* (1995). I particularly cherish A.L. Morton's *The English Utopia*, which was first published in 1952.

'Revisionism', or rather revisionisms, for I will be suggesting that there was more than one sort of revisionism, originated in the wake of the 'Gentry Controversy' of the 1950s and 1960s.[1] The demolition of R.H. Tawney's thesis on 'The Rise of the Gentry' led to an intensive, wide-ranging and prolonged re-thinking of the causes of the English Revolution. Tawney was not a Marxist but Christopher Hill's Marxist interpretation was allied with Tawney's thesis and explained the civil war as a conflict between progressive landowners benefiting from economic changes, which carried with them the development of capitalism, and conservative landowners unable or unwilling to profit from those changes and so tending to decline economically. Refutations of Tawney's work merged with refutations of Hill's interpretation. It was widely assumed that the Marxist interpretation of the English civil war as a bourgeois revolution had collapsed, and indeed all social change explanations of the English Revolution.[2] Conrad Russell announced in 1973 that 'social change explanations of the English civil war must be regarded as having broken down'.[3]

In the re-thinking that followed it was not only social change explanations that were swept aside but also the long-established explanations in terms of constitutional and religious conflicts. The latter, which had been dominant since the monumental work of the nineteenth-century historian S.R. Gardiner, had explained the civil war as the result of a period of conflict over the constitution and religion between the king and parliaments. Tawneyite and Marxist historians had sought to relate that conflict to long-term social changes. Thus revisionists attacked on a broad front the view that the English Revolution had long-term constitutional causes and the view that it was the result of long-term social changes, and so embracing the interpretations of both Gardiner and Hill. Conrad Russell judged 'that both the types of explanation favoured over the past forty years, based on long-term constitutional conflict and on long-term social change respectively, appear to have suffered irretrievable breakdown: we have to begin all over again'. He denied that he had 'abolished the long-term causes of the civil war': 'Unlike some colleagues, I see no *a priori* impossibility in this type of explanation, but it remains highly improbable'.[4]

## Hindsight and anachronism

The revisionists objected to the 'hindsight' which read backwards the civil war into earlier periods, seeing everything that did or did not happen from the Reformation of the sixteenth century onwards in the light of a supposed eventual outcome in 1640 and 1642. They protested that instead of earlier periods being studied in their own terms they were distorted by the pursuit of preconceived notions of the causes of the English Revolution, such as Lawrence Stone's non-Marxist, sociologically inspired survey which arranged the 'causes' of the English Revolution as 'preconditions, 1529–1629', 'precipitants, 1629–1639', and 'triggers, 1640–2'.[5] But this left the revisionists with problems about explaining the outbreak of the civil war, since it appeared that its causes were to be confined to a few months before October 1642.

Revisionists criticised 'anachronisms' — the importing into the seventeenth century of concepts and preconceptions derived from later centuries, such as Marxist ideas of 'class' and 'revolution' which were said to be applicable only to the nineteenth and twentieth centuries, and assimilating the English Revolution to the French Revolution. But inevitably the revisionists imported into the seventeenth century their own concepts and preconceptions derived from Britain in the 1970s and 1980s.

The explanation of the crisis of 1640–2 as the climax of constitutional conflicts, which had long been developing, was ruled out: 'In the first place, it now appears possible to say that the civil war was undoubtedly not the culmination of a struggle for power between king and parliament'.[6] Alongside the work of Russell on parliaments, another contributory stream of revisionism was the work of Nicholas Tyacke on the church. In a seminal article in 1973 he argued that the crisis of 1640–2 was not the outcome of the development of a puritan movement over several decades seeking to reform the church and society, as non-Marxist and Marxist historians had maintained.[7]

> Hindsight is often the curse of the historian, and none more so in attempting to reconstruct the religious history of the pre-civil war era. The battle lines of 1640–2 were not drawn by the early 1620s in this any more than other spheres.

There was a consensus in the church in the early seventeenth century rather than a split between 'Anglicans' (an anachronistic term) and 'Puritans', but this was broken in the late 1620s and the 1630s by Charles I and Archbishop Laud. There was a 'counter-revolution' attempted from above, seeking a retreat from the Calvinist theology which had held sway until then, and imposing ceremonies and practices which were regarded as 'innovations', and pointing in the direction of 'popery'. The reaction to this was conservative, not revolutionary, and a desire to preserve the church as it had evolved under Elizabeth I and James I. The Laudian innovations were removed by the Long Parliament in 1640–2.[8] It was not until the latter period that there emerged demands, not just for a return to the status quo of 1559–1625, but beyond that for further and radical reformation, notably the abolition of episcopacy. It cannot be said, therefore, that the religious policies of Charles and Laud caused the civil war, because those policies had been dismantled before the civil war, and many of those who had opposed those policies supported the king in the civil war. From that it would follow that the religious conflicts in the civil war were generated between 1640 and 1642 and had no long-term causes, though that leaves something of a mystery as to the origins of the radical religious outbursts, especially since they involved pressure on parliament by popular preachers, petitions and demonstrations.

## Revisionist interpretations

There is no revisionist school or clique, and the revisionists disagree amongst themselves, but in general terms there has emerged the following features in the picture of the background to the English civil war: there were no deep issues of constitutional principle, no struggle for power between king and parliament, and no aim to alter the constitution by making parliament, specifically the House of Commons, supreme; the importance of the House of Commons had been exaggerated and the importance of the House of lords underestimated, and the political conflicts that did arise were often generated by struggles within the king's government and court between aristocratic factions, subsequently reflected in parliament. For example, in one of the founding essays of revisionism, Kevin Sharpe concluded a study of the Earl of Arundel and 'his circle' in 1618–28:

> Historians have singled out the 1620s as the decade of issues and conflict. The political activities of Arundel and his circle during these years suggest rather the importance of personalities and personal connections — not connections based on constitutional principles or ideological commitments nor connections founded on the mere pursuit of office, but connections strengthened by traditional beliefs about correct behaviour and modes of action, about methods not policies. The Arundel circle is a case-study in the values and politics of Renaissance England.[9]

As with much revisionist history the negative arguments are more persuasive than the positive conclusions. I am not surprised that studies confined to the governing class find broad areas of consensus in ways of thinking and acting, but I would add that this class is likely to be divided by struggles for place, power and profit, intertwined with differences over policies.

The preferred method of the revisionists is detailed, chronological, political narratives of a short period of time, rather than broad analytical and thematic surveys on a long time-scale. The choice of the former approach may build in an assumption against long-term causes, while the choice of the latter may build in the opposite assumption. The revisionist approach may be exemplified by Conrad Russell's *Parliaments and English Politics 1621–9* (1979) and Anthony Fletcher's *The Outbreak of the English Civil War* (1981), the latter covering two years in 422 pages.

Revisionists, of course, reject Marxist interpretations, but often by simply ignoring them or dismissing them out-of-hand, and indeed they may not have read them, for they assume that Marxism means a crude economic determinism. But the main objective of revisionist historians is to dispose of the notion that the English civil war was a class struggle. There was nothing new about that, however, they merely took over well-known anti-Marxist views. Fletcher asserted: 'Nor, it has been established, can the war be explained in terms of social revolution: the ultimate split was quite clearly a split within the governing class'.[10] 'There is little evidence that the English civil war began as a social conflict', wrote John Morrill: 'The gentry were divided down the middle: attempts to distinguish the allegiance of greater and lesser gentry, rising and declining gentry, ancient and *arriviste* gentry, office-holding and "mere" gentry have largely failed'.[11] Russell recovered well from the hurt of discovering this: 'it has become painfully clear that it is impossible to interpret the civil war as the clash of two clearly differentiated social groups or classes: the fullest possible knowledge of men's social and economic background ... tells us nothing about their likely allegiance in the civil war'.[12]

## Marxist reappraisals

It is important to observe, however, that 'revisionism' in the wake of the 'Gentry Controversy' was not confined to non-Marxist historians, but that there was a reappraisal of Marxist interpretation. Christopher Hill added in the conclusion to a volume of essays which he published in 1974: 'In particular the Marxist conception of a bourgeois revolution, which I find the most helpful model for understanding the English Revolution, does not mean a revolution made by the bourgeoisie'. He quoted Isaac Deutscher in support.[13] He elaborated this in 1980 in an essay entitled 'A Bourgeois Revolution?': 'So in discussing whether the English Revolution was a bourgeois revolution or not we must begin by defining terms ... The phrase in Marxist usage does not mean a revolution made by or consciously willed by the bourgeoisie:

> The English Revolution, like all revolutions, was caused by the breakdown of the old society; it was brought about neither by the wishes of the bourgeoisie, nor by the leaders of the Long Parliament. But its outcome was the establishment of conditions far more favourable to the development of capitalism than those which prevailed before 1640.

The hypothesis is that this outcome, and the Revolution itself, were made possible by the fact there had already been a considerable development of capitalist relations in England, but that it was the structures, fractures, and pressures of the society, rather than the wishes of leaders, which dictated the outbreak of revolution and shaped the state which emerged from it. 'We should not think of "the bourgeoisie" as a self-conscious class.' 'There was no direct takeover of power by "the bourgeoisie".' 'Nobody, then willed the English Revolution: it happened. But if we look at its outcome what emerged was a state in which the administrative organs that most impeded capitalist development had been abolished.'[14]

Hill's reference to 'the structures, fractures, and pressures of the society' remains somewhat vague and it is uncertain how they relate to the outcome. 'By 1640 the social forces let loose by or accompanying the rise of capitalism, especially in agriculture, could no longer be contained within the old political framework....' How does that (whatever it may mean: enclosures? Consolidation of farms? Production for the market by exploitation of wage-labour?) relate to the next statement: 'What mattered in the English Revolution was that the ruling class was deeply divided at a time when there was much combustible material among the lower classes normally excluded from politics'. Was it 'the rise of capitalism' that divided the ruling class, if so, how? The combustion that took place was in London and the cloth-making districts, not in agriculture, and its ultimate outcome was to reunite the ruling class.[15]

Norah Carlin mounted a vigorous defence of the Marxist interpretation of the English Revolution as a bourgeois revolution, complete with a leading role for part of the bourgeoisie of merchants and manufacturers.[16] Hill's interpretation of the English bourgeois revolution was endorsed in an article by Alex Callinicos, which, while usefully embracing different forms of bourgeois revolution, said specifically of the English and French Revolutions:

> The main thrust of the revisionist critique challenges the idea that the bourgeoisie as a class led either the English or the French Revolutions ... The revisionist claim is, however, damaging to classical Marxism only on condition that we conceive bourgeois revolutions as necessarily the result of the self-conscious action of the capitalist class. Such a view has often been defended by Marxists — indeed by Marx himself ... Responding to the revisionist attacks requires a shift in focus. Bourgeois revolutions must be understood, not as revolutions consciously made by capitalists, but as revolutions which promote capitalism'.[17]

It seems then that it is not a difficulty for the Marxist interpretation that there were nobles, gentry, yeoman farmers, merchants and craftsmen on both sides in the English civil war, which was not a class struggle, just as the revisionists said. The bourgeoisie evaporated from the English Revolution and so did the class struggle, except insofar as there was a struggle of poor peasants and artisans against capitalist developments.

Non-Marxist and anti-Marxist revisionists, however, could not evade the fact that there was a civil war (in which it is estimated 190,000 people died in England and Wales out of a population of five million),[18] and that in 1649 the king was publicly tried and executed, the monarchy and the House of Lords were abolished, and a republic was established. Morrill was troubled by the questions of his students about how in the light of revisionism such outcomes could be explicable.[19] The problem for the revisionists was that, however persuasive and successful their work of demolition, and indeed because of their success in overturning previous explanations, they could not explain why there was a civil war or 'Great Rebellion' (they disliked the term 'revolution'), and they were sensitive to the jibe that they had proved the civil war did not happen. But religion lay at hand to answer their problem. There was, of course, nothing new about that. Morrill had said as long ago as 1976: 'What emerges quite clearly from a study of the activists in the summer of 1642 ... is that, for them, religion was the crucial issue'.[20] He held to this consistently: 'If there were profound differences between the two sides, they were over religion'.[21] Fletcher concluded his book on the outbreak of the civil war with the statement: 'There is a real sense in which the English civil war was a war of religion'.[22]

## Religion

In 1984 Morrill published an article on 'The Religious Context of the English Civil War'. He saw the struggle as being between two small minorities which were motivated to fight by 'the force of religion': 'The English civil war was not the first European revolution: it was the last of the Wars of Religion'.[23] Barry Coward welcomed the revival of an interpretation which could explain both the outbreak of the civil war and the train of events that led to 1649:

> It is heartening, therefore, that the very latest work on the Revolution amounts to a welcome reassertion of a 'revolutionary' strand: the importance of religion as a ideological force that helped to impel events in a radical direction in the 1640s. Research by both Anthony Fletcher and John Morrill indicates that ... what set the two sides apart was religious

commitment: in the case of the royalists, commitment to the kind of church that had developed between 1559 and 1625 [before the Laudian regime] and, in the case of the parliamentarians, commitment to the cause of a puritan 'godly reformation'.

Fear of lower-class religious radicalism backed by popular demonstrations, and fear that attacks on hierarchy in the church would spill over into attacks on hierarchy in society, helped to propel some men to take arms for the king, and fear of 'popish' plots impelled others to take arms for parliament, fearing the king and his allies could not be trusted to keep out 'popery'.[24]

When Morrill in 1993 defended his article, he illuminated revisionist perceptions:

> I can now see that the deployment of the term 'England's Wars of Religion', was a quintessentially revisionist statement. By locating the mid-seventeenth-century crisis in an early modern context away from what I took to be misleading and unhelpful comparisons with modern revolutions from 1789 on, I was seeking to reject a fundamentally anachronistic approach to the seventeenth century, one designed to render the event explicable by assimilating it to a category familiar to modern experience and social theory. [The article] was an essential part of the revisionist claim for the particularity of past experience, and for the gulf between our mental world and that of the seventeenth century. Thus I was consciously seeking to assimilate the events in seventeenth-century England to a class of events which belong distinctively to the period under study and not to the social and secular divisions alleged to underlie most modern revolution.[25]

But it is possible that there was a 'mental gulf' between the world of the mid-seventeenth century and the world of the late sixteenth-century wars of religion. Morrill seems in danger of falling into the heresy of long termism, seeing 'England's Wars of Religion' bubbling under the surface since Elizabeth's reign, and he certainly commits the sin of anachronism because the Wars of Religion were between Catholics and Protestants and the English civil war was between Protestants. He followed the revisionist line in eliminating constitutional conflict as the cause of the civil war. 'It is my contention that what made civil war possible in 1642 was a crisis in religion', he wrote: religion 'proved to have the ideological dynamism to drive minorities to arms: the momentum of "constitutionalist" argument in 1642 was not sufficient'. He denied that he was giving a monocausal explanation of the civil war and said that he 'never thought or claimed that the crisis of the 1640s was "only" about religion'. But he agreed that the influence of religious commitment was not as 'straightforward' amongst the royalists as amongst the parliamentarians: '... many royalists may have put allegiance to the Established Church second' to personal loyalty to the king and fear of the social consequences of the parliamentarian cause.[26]

Religion, sanitised from politics and class, seems to be regarded as an alternative to Marxist interpretations. That was the message which Coward got from the works of Fletcher and Morrill:

> the common feature of those who committed themselves, whether to the king or parliament, in 1642 was not social class, geographical origins or divergent attitudes to the constitution ... What set the two sides apart was religious commitment.[27]

But Peter Lake made the obvious point that in early modern England religious, political and social attitudes were closely interwoven: the choice between king and parliament involved a choice 'between two competing sets of social and political, as well as religious, priorities and values'.[28]

Once the social is re-introduced into interpretations historians look again at 'social change' explanations. Interestingly, Conrad Russell left open this possibility in his 1973 statement:

> It is possible that a new social change explanation may hereafter be constructed ... In so far as there was a general social change in the century before the civil war, it was not in the position of the gentry or the peerage, but in the rise of many of the upper yeomanry ... Even if the merchant class as a whole was not rising, there were certainly many tradesmen and artificers ... who were also rising. These were the sort of people who provided much of the backbone of those truly revolutionary movements the New Model Army and the Leveller movement. These people did not belong to what were normally regarded as the political classes, but without strong support from among them, parliament would not have been able to win its first crucial victory by frightening the king out of London in January 1642. Any new social change explanation will have to be based on the power of these people, most of whom were rising, not so much at the expense of the gentry, as at the expense of smallholders and the labouring poor.[29]

## The 'middling sort'

At the start I noted that the influence of revisionism was matched by the growth of 'history from below'. The latter proved to be the basis for a 'new social change explanation', in terms of the yeomen (better-off farmers) and independent artisans — 'the middle sort of people', as they were called at the time. In 1987 Tim Harris spoke of the 'rediscovery of the middling sort'.[30] In 1988 Barry Reay introduced a book of essays on popular culture in seventeenth-century England with the statement:

> This book does not deal with the peerage and gentry of the rural areas of early modern England or the pseudo-gentry and wealthy merchants of the towns ... In many respects the seventeenth century is the century of the middling sort.

They ranged from yeoman farmers to prosperous tradesmen and craftsmen. They became literate; they dominated many local communities as churchwardens, overseers of the poor, and jurymen; some of them joined radical religious sects and radical political movements like the Levellers; 'they petitioned, demonstrated and agitated in London ... forcing the pace of the English Revolution'.[31] In 1994 a whole book of essays was devoted to 'The Middling Sort of People' in England, but in their introduction the editors pointed out a defect in 'history from below' which handicapped its ability to explain events like the English Revolution:

> Following the lead of E.P. Thompson [historians] have committed themselves to history from below, and thus to a focus on society in terms of a polarization between the élite and the people. Pre-occupied with the interplay between the ruling élite and the lower classes ... they have shown little interest in distinguishing amongst the people between the middling sort and the rest (with the honourable exceptions of Manning and Hill). Both by adopting the polarized vocabularies of élite and popular (or patrician and plebeian), and by the themes they have chosen for analysis, they have tended to obscure any distinctive role for a middling sort.[32]

Hill stressed the role of the 'middling sort' in important essays in 1981 and 1988.[33] Morrill gave due and critical attention to 'the yeomen and the rural and urban artisans — the "middling sorts",' and recognized that this called into question 'the assumption that it is the gentry alone who determined the political alignments of a county in the civil war':

A good deal of recent work has shown a growing self-confidence and independence in the attitudes and behaviour of substantial yeoman-farmers, craftsmen and so on. The substitution of the parish for the manor as the principal unit of local government represents a transfer of effective authority from the generality of tenants and freeholders to an aristocracy of wealthy farmers and craftsmen, and it is clear that such men could and did wield considerable authority over the poor and rootless ... Interpretations of allegiance which rest content with analyses of gentry activity are thus inadequate, and have been directly attacked by Brian Manning and Joyce Malcolm. Their work makes it obvious that the 'middling sort' were capable of independent action and that many did not wait upon the gentry's decisions. Similarly, the idea that the labourers, cottagers and others blindly followed their landlords' and masters' lead needs important qualification.[34]

The split in the ruling class of course remains a precondition of the outbreak of the revolution, and it is still vital to explain that. But, with the exception of Robert Brenner, we no longer search amongst the aristocracy and gentry to find the bourgeoisie. The 'middle sort of people' were independent small producers — they owned or possessed the means of production and were not wage-earners but employers of labour — they constituted a class in the Marxist sense. Maurice Dobb's work becomes again a seminal text, with its analysis of the role of the small producers in the transition from feudalism to capitalism.[35] A focus on the 'middling sort' means that the impact of long-term social change and the growth of capitalism again become central concerns. Brenner's view is that capitalism developed in England from the end of the medieval period within a landlord framework by means of the self-transformation of the feudal aristocracy into a capitalist class. But Patricia Croot and David Parker argue against this by stressing the process of differentiation within the ranks of the English peasantry, which produced the yeomanry. The engrossing of holdings into larger farms was not just down to manorial lords but was made possible by there being peasant farmers who were making profits and had the capital to invest in larger holdings. By mid-seventeenth-century in England there were more larger farmers employing wage labour to produce for the market. Brenner's thesis fails to focus on the capitalist farmers and the capitalist employers in manufacture, whose roles may have been decisive from the early sixteenth century to the mid-seventeenth century in shifting the economy towards capitalism.[36] The 'middling sort' faced two ways: on the one hand they struggled with the aristocrats and big city merchants for a larger political role, and on the other hand they strove to control and discipline the wage-earners and the poor in general. Exploitation and class conflicts again become central concerns in interpreting the English Revolution.

In relation to the outbreak and course of the revolution Morrill concludes that 'it would be surprising if in fact the role of the "middling sort" is decisive, for it seems likely that the "middling sort" were as divided as were the gentry'.[37] It is an undoubted fact that the 'middling sort' were divided, politically and religiously. It is also an undoubted fact that some of the 'middling sort' were, or were becoming, capitalist farmers and capitalist manufacturers, while many were sinking towards becoming wage-earners. A bourgeois class and a proletarian class was in process of formation, and the English Revolution took place within that framework. But it must be stressed that there are many disputed and unresolved questions about how far or in what ways political and religious divisions within the 'middling sort' related to economic divisions, and the weight to be attached to the role of the bourgeoisie emerging from the 'middling sort' in the outbreak and outcome of the English Revolution.

## Conclusions

I would like to offer the following general observations. The fact that the whole of a class is not on one side in a conflict (something which it may be said never happens) does not mean that it is not a class conflict. All the aristocracy did not support the king but those who did so were motivated by their sense of the interests of their class, as they themselves made plain; all the small producers did not support parliament, but those who did so were motivated by their sense of the interests of their class, as their spokesmen made clear. Marxist interpretations are regarded as being refuted when each party is shown to have been composed of a coalition of different social groups or classes, but that does not preclude each of those elements being motivated by its own identity and mentality, and its own sense of the needs of its social group or class, while finding for a time a correspondence of interests with other groups or classes. But as the struggle develops in the ensuing phase differences clarify and sharpen: more aristocrats rally to monarchy and episcopacy as instruments to defend their class, and the contradictions between the 'middling sort' and the labouring poor become evident. The outcome of the revolution is shaped by changing class alignments and class conflicts. If these observations are correct the case against the English civil war being a class struggle, and against the English Revolution being moulded by class struggle, is seriously weakened.

The best commemoration of A.L. Morton is that *Class Struggle in the English Revolution* is alive and kicking.

## Notes

1. Christopher Hill, 'Parliament and People in Seventeenth-Century England', *Past and Present*, No.92 (1981) p.101; J.P. Sommerville, *Politics and Ideology in England, 1603–1640* (London, 1986), pp.1–2.
2. J.H. Hexter, *Reappraisals in History* (London, 1961); Lawrence Stone, 'The Social Origins of the English Revolution', *Causes of the English Revolution 1529–1642* (London, 1972).
3. Conrad Russell (ed.), *The Origins of the English Civil War* (London, 1973), pp.6–9.
4. Conrad Russell, 'The British Problem and the English Civil War', *History*, Vol.72, No.236 (1987), p.396.
5. Stone, *Causes*.
6. Conrad Russell, *Parliaments and English Politics 1621–1629* (Oxford, 1979), p.426.
7. William Haller, *The Rise of Puritanism* (New York, 1938); Christopher Hill, *Society and Puritanism in Pre–Revolutionary England* (London, 1964).
8. Nicholas Tyacke, 'Puritanism, Arminianism and Counter-Revolution', in Russell (ed.), *Origins*.
9. Kevin Sharpe, 'The Earl of Arundel, His Circle and the Opposition to the Duke of Buckingham, 1618–1628', in Kevin Sharpe (ed.), *Faction and Parliament: essays in early Stuart History* (Oxford, 1978), p.244.
10. Anthony Fletcher, *The Outbreak of the English Civil War* (London, 1981), p.407.
11. John Morrill (ed.), *Reactions to the English Civil War 1642–1649* (London, 1982), p.9.
12. Conrad Russell, *The Causes of the English Civil War* (Oxford, 1990), p.2.
13. Christopher Hill, *Change and Continuity in Seventeenth-Century England* (London, 1974), pp.279–80.
14. Christopher Hill, 'A Bourgeois Revolution?', in J.G.A. Pocock (ed.), *Three British Revolutions: 1641, 1688, 1776* (Princeton, 1980), pp.110–11, 129, 131, 134. In the preface to a new edition of *The Good Old Cause* (1969) Hill said: 'Bourgeois revolution signifies a revolution which — whatever the subjective intention of the revolutionaries — had the effect of establishing conditions favourable to the development of capitalism'. In 'The place of the Seventeenth-Century Revolution in English History', *A Nation of Change and Novelty* (London, 1990), he wrote: 'The revolution was not planned, not willed', pp.18–19.
15. Hill, 'A Bourgeois Revolution?', pp.112, 124.
16. Norah Carlin, 'Marxism and the English Civil War', *International Socialism*, No.10 (1980–1).

17. Alex Callinicos, 'Bourgeois revolutions and historical materialism', *International Socialism*, No.43 (1989), pp.113–27.
18. Charles Carlton, *Going to the Wars: The experience of the British civil wars, 1638–1651* (London, 1994), pp.211, 214.
19. Morrill, *Reactions*, p.1.
20. J.S. Morrill, *The Revolt of the Provinces: Conservatives and radicals in the English civil war 1630–1650* (London, 1976), p.47.
21. Morrill, *Reactions*, p.15.
22. Fletcher, *Outbreak*, pp.417–18.
23. John Morrill, 'The Religious Context of the English Civil War', *Transactions of the Royal Historical Society*, 5th series Vol.34 (1984), pp.157, 176–8.
24. Barry Coward, 'Was there an English Revolution in the Middle of the Seventeenth Century?', in Colin Jones, Malyn Newitt and Stephen Roberts (eds), *Politics and People in Revolutionary England* (Oxford, 1986), pp.29–30.
25. John Morrill, *The Nature of the English Revolution* (London, 1993), pp.33–45.
26. Morrill, *Nature*, pp.33–45, 69–70.
27. Coward, 'Was there an English Revolution?', pp.29–30.
28. Peter Lake, 'Anti-Popery: The structure of a prejudice', in Richard Cust and Ann Hughes (eds), *Conflict in Early Stuart England* (London, 1989), p.97.
29. Russell (ed.), *Origins*, pp.8–9.
30. Tim Harris, *London Crowds in the Reign of Charles II* (Cambridge, 1987), p.18.
31. Barry Reay (ed.), *Popular Culture in Seventeenth-Century England* (London, 1985), p.1.
32. Jonathan Barry and Christopher Brooks (eds), *The Middling Sort of People: Culture, Society and Politics in England 1550–1800* (London, 1994), p.10.
33. Christopher Hill, 'Parliament and People', pp.111–12, 118–22; 'The Poor and the People in Seventeenth-Century England', in Frederick Krantz (ed.), *History from Below: studies in popular protest and popular ideology* (Oxford, 1988) pp.43–4.
34. Morrill, *Reactions*, pp.10–11. He is referring to Brian Manning, *The English People and the English Revolution* (1976; new edn London, 1991), and J.L. Malcolm, *Caesar's Due: Loyalty and King Charles 1642–1646* (London, 1983).
35. Maurice Dobb, *Studies in the Development of Capitalism* (London, 1946); Rodney Hilton (ed.), *The Transition from Feudalism to Capitalism* (London, 1976).
36. T.H. Aston and C.H.E. Philpin (eds), *The Brenner Debate: Agrarian class structure and economic development in pre-industrial Europe* (London, 1985), pp.79–90.
37. Morrill, *Reactions*, pp.10–11.

# Popular Historiography in the Second World War
A Critique of *Narrating the Thirties*

## Roger Spalding

In 1996 John Baxendale and Christopher Pawling published *Narrating the Thirties: 1930 to the Present*. They argue that history is not simply the past but is a cultural construct, or narrative, that changes from period to period. Hence, they argue, perceptions of the 1930s vary from decade to decade. Narrative changes, it is claimed, are the products of the needs of the present not of new discoveries about the past.

> This continual re-presentation of 'the Thirties' ... owes more to forces at work in the present than to any improvements in our knowledge of the past.[1]

Broadly speaking they argue that a negative view of the 1930s predominated until 1979, a view represented by such works as Branson and Heinemann's *Britain in the 1930s*. The turning point came in 1979 with the publication of Cook and Stevenson's work *The Slump*. According to Baxendale and Pawling it was the emphasis of Cook and Stevenson's book that made it an historiographical watershed. Unlike Branson and Heinemann, both long-term members of the Communist Party, Cook and Stevenson stressed the moderation and stability evident in Britain in the 1930s. This book was, say Baxendale and Pawling, an historical response to the political turmoil and extremism in 1970s Britain; it was a re-affirmation of the durability of British institutions.

### Popular historiography

A central part of Baxendale and Pawling's argument is that during the course of the Second World War a popular historiographic battle took place which was largely won by the political Left, and which resulted in the establishment of the pessimistic interpretation of the 1930s as an orthodoxy.

In essence as time went on there took shape two versions of what the war meant and how and why it was being fought, and each was important in mobilising the support of the population. Both were formed early in the war, and both persisted into the post-war era as powerful, and to some extent rival, national myths: myths, not because they were necessarily untrue, but because their main significance was how they were used in the present, rather than their truth to past reality.

The Churchillian myth portrayed a nation united under its great leader, Winston Churchill. It evoked a thousand years of unbroken history, a national mythology of the Island Race, standing alone against foreign enemies (the Spanish Armada, Napoleon), slow to rouse but proud and heroic in the defence of its freedom. This version of the war, with its appeal to history and to patriotism, is heard in Churchill's wartime oratory as much in its high-flown tone and language as in what it actually says: 'Upon this battle depends the survival of Christian civilisation. Upon it depends our own British life and the long continuity of our institutions and our Empire. Let us therefore brace ourselves to our duty, and so bear ourselves that if the British Empire and its Commonwealth last for a thousand years, men will say this was their finest hour.' Note the emphasis on timeless unities (Christian civilisation, British life), on history, continuity, duty, the Empire: all delivered in the cadences of a Shakespearean actor, or perhaps, an Anglican bishop. Note too the lack of any reference to recent history, or to the personal experience of the audience.

The other myth was populist and democratic: the People's War. The war was being fought, not for patriotic duty or past glories, but by and for the common people of England, the kindly, decent, patient folk of this country, as J.B. Priestley put it, who deserve so much better than they have had, and for whom a nobler frame-work of life must be constructed after they had made the sacrifice that war demands.[2]

Hence according to this view Churchillian Conservatism emphasised timeless unities, whilst the People's War mythology concentrated upon the recent experience of the pre-war period. It is this part of their analysis that will now be discussed.

Before examining the issues raised by these claims it is necessary to point to a certain problem within Baxendale and Pawling's analysis. Clearly it is beyond dispute that during the War a great deal of broadly anti-Conservative material appeared, much of which concentrated upon the poor record of the Tories in the inter-war period. *Guilty Men*, written by

Michael Foot, Frank Owen and Peter Howard, and published in the immediate aftermath of Dunkirk as an attack on the government's re-armament programme, sold over a quarter of a million copies. Other pamphlets in the same series, published by Gollancz, sold over 100,000 copies. The problem with Baxendale and Pawling's analysis is the inference they draw from these anti-conservative publications, the claim they make that this kind of material actually re-shaped popular consciousness. 'The dominance of these negative views of the Thirties thus both reflected and helped to constitute the ideological ascendency of the centre-Left during the 1940s.'[3]

This is a very large claim and one that is difficult to actually support with concrete evidence. As will be shown the claim that publications reflect popular consciousness can be used to undermine their arguments.

On a very basic level it is possible to simply refute their claims that Conservatives did not address the immediate pre-war past. The 1939 Korda Brothers film, *The Lion Has Wings*, addressed the inter-war period in a very direct and, from a modern perspective, unexpected fashion. The opening sequences of this propaganda film have three elements. First, the audience is shown images of the essential England that is under threat. This is a rural, southern and historic England, constituted by the White Cliffs of Dover, half-timbered houses, ancient cathedrals, and Oxbridge colleges. Second the audience is shown images of modern flats, schools and hospitals, which, the voice-over states, represent the great social advances made in Britain in the immediate pre-war period. Third the film contrasts the British national character with that of the Germans. The British, the film claims, enjoy pacific pastimes, like cricket and other forms of sport, whereas the Germans prefer military parades and a vigorous goose-step. King George VI is shown singing, with the appropriate actions, *Under the Spreading Chestnut Tree*. Hitler is shown addressing a mass rally at Nuremberg. The message is clear, the British are decent, peace-loving folk, the Germans are mindless, militaristic robots.[4] Taken together the opening sequences combine timeless unities, like historic rural England and the essential decency of the British with a very positive view of the immediate past. The Kordas, who acted as advisers to the Conservative Party on film propaganda, in this film presented their own version of the People's War, a version that stressed what the People stood to lose in the war, rather than what they ought to gain at the end of it.

The opening sequences of *The Lion Has Wings* addressed domestic issues, Quintin Hogg's 1945 pamphlet, *The Left Was Never Right*, addressed issues of foreign policy. Hogg accepted that the politicians of the inter-war period had made mistakes, albeit from the best possible motives.

> Between 1919 and 1939 this country was governed by a series of statesmen of the very highest character, men of idealism, constitutional yet progressive, internationally minded yet patriotic, courteous, well-cultivated, kind but in the main neither clear-headed nor politically inspired. They loved peace and would not prepare for war. They hated war so much that they were not prepared until the very last moment to set the great resources of this country in motion against wrong, and in the end they were compelled to embark on the greatest conflict in the history of the planet.[5]

## Conservative interpretations

Hogg also claimed that the pacificism of the Labour Party made it partly responsible for the lack of military preparedness. To protect peace in the future Hogg argued that a new international order, based upon an armed alliance of the great powers, was required. So, like *The Lion Has Wings*, Hogg does engage with the immediate past, and he also looks to the future, connecting both past and future with eternal unities.

> For what are the nations which most influenced the history and destiny of human kind? Not Babylon, but Jerusalem. Not Macedon, but Athens. Not wealthy Carthage, but frugal Rome. From these three small Mediterranean cities have come the religion, the tradition of political freedom, and the respect for law which are the chief excellences of Western civilisation. To these three a fourth name must now be added. It is the name of a little island in the North Atlantic.here is a people rich in genius, free and independent, yet patient of discipline, brave and fearless, but not aggressive, practical yet not materialistic, a nation of craftsmen and scientists still capable of poetry, of political genius still sustaining military ardour, the home of technical discovery wherein the rule of righteousness is no less pursued than material advantage.[6]

Britain as the fourth pillar of Western civilisation? For Hogg the essential features of the national character would overcome the mistakes of the inter-war period, and carry Britain through to a significant role in the post-war world. Clearly, here too there is no separation between perceptions of the immediate and distant past.

Taken on their own *The Lion Has Wings* and *The Left Was Never Right* could be seen as exceptional items in a sea of Left-leaning material denigrating the 1930s. Is it possible to find evidence that has a direct relationship with a mass audience? Curiously for self-proclaimed cultural historians Baxendale and Pawling do not consider the popular, commercial cinema. By 1941 there was a weekly cinema audience of 20 million plus in Great Britain, an audience whose preferences one might expect to find reflected, to use Baxendale and Pawling's term, in the films on offer. There are films that support their analysis. The conclusion of the 1941 production of *Love on the Dole* shows Mrs Hardcastle looking into the middle distance and making a heartfelt plea for a better future. This was very different from the deeply pessimistic conclusion of the original 1933 novel. Although the film is set in the 1930s it is obviously a contribution to the wartime discourse of 'Never Again'. On the other hand there was a whole genre of film that quite definitely validated Britain's existing social structure. War has been described as the ultimate test of a society, in the twentieth century the test results take the form of feature films.

## Popular cinema

The 1942 film, *In Which We Serve*, opens in 1939. It shows Captain Kinross (Noel Coward) taking over command of a newly commissioned destroyer, *HMS Torrin*, and it also shows us a view of Kinross's home life. He is chauffeured from the ship to his large country house, he takes cocktails with his wife (Celia Johnson) before dinner — cook has promised something special — and he demonstrates a magnificently stiff upper lip: responding to his wife's query 'Will there be a war darling?' with 'Yes I think there will', delivered without a flicker of emotion or apparent concern. Kinross is obviously extremely well-off, hardly surprising since the character was based on Lord Mountbatten. During the course of the film which also focuses on an Able Seaman and a Petty Officer (the working and lower middle class, respectively) Kinross proves to be an inspiring figure able, without any irony, to tell the survivors of his crew, after the *Torrin* has been sunk: 'Now she lies in 1500 fathoms and with her more than half our shipmates. If they had to die, what a grand way to go.'

*HMS Torrin* can be seen as *HMS Great Britain*. It shows the British population united and inspired by the clipped vowels of one of Britain's natural leaders. The implicit historical message is that the upper classes of the inter-war period are essentially sound and war-winners. This is a mythology for the masses that displays them, with one cowardly exception, as the faithful followers of their social superiors. *We Dive At Dawn*, also made in 1942, shows a similar social hierarchy. The captain of the submarine, *Sea Tiger* (John Mills) telephones his butler to arrange a string of social engagements for his seven-day leave. While one of the featured crew members an Able Seaman returns home to discover his wife has left him and fled to the security of her brother's chip shop. Again the film demonstrates a range of social classes united in the war-effort under the leadership of somebody with the right sort of accent.

In the 1945 film, *The Way to the Stars*, we see Pilot-Officer Penrose (John Mills) and Acting Squadron-Leader Archdale (Michael Redgrave) at the controls, in all senses, loyally assisted by the proletarian gunner, Nobby (Bill Owen). *The Way to the Stars* is also interesting because it consciously places the Second World War within a long historical perspective. The film opens with a series of shots of a derelict airfield, just after the end of the war. As the camera moves across the scene a flock of sheep with their shepherd come into view, they, in turn, lead the camera past a slab of rock embedded in the ground. The slab indicates that this is Halfpenny Field. This information is confirmed by the voice-over which also states that Halfpenny Field was mentioned in the Domesday Book. The subliminal message is clear, the Second World War was fought to maintain this timeless, rural England. The same message is confirmed in a later sequence that shows a squadron of Blenheims setting out to bomb German invasion barges — the action is taking place in 1940. As they make their way to the Channel coast they pass over the market town of Shepley, with its medieval church, its Georgian coaching inn and ancient market cross. We last see the squadron from the perspective of a pair of fly fishermen. This then is the England to be protected from invasion, the ancient, rural Southern England of gentle rolling hills and chalk streams.

The defenders of this essential England were the products of the public schools. The Second World War, like the Battle of Waterloo, was won, according to British film-makers, on the playing fields of Eton, and a host of other public schools. A traditional England protected and saved by its traditional rulers, this is the 'mythology' of many British war films.

This genre of film, with its essentially conservative message, continued to be popular well into the 1950s. In *The Cruel Sea*, made in 1953, Stanley Baker appears as the First Lieutenant on the featured destroyer. He is clearly not a gent — not the type that one could enjoy a pink gin with in the wardroom. Fortunately, an addiction to the proletarian delights of fried sausages — 'snorkers' — leads to him being carried off with a stomach complaint. Donald Sinden and Jack Hawkins subsequently set sail knowing, as does the audience, that the right chaps are in command. In *The Colditz Story* (1955) the upper middle-class British prisoners turn their escape attempts into public schoolboy 'japes', they even use schoolboy slang, describing the German commander as 'Matron' and long-term prisoners as 'old boys'. Their principal grievance against their German captors appears to be that they are of inferior social status, they are 'horrid little men'. Within the British war film there was an in-built conservatism which sets out how traditional British institutions overcame Nazism and how Britain's 'natural' upper middle-class rulers proved more than up to the demands of the war-effort. These films were enormously popular, more so, even, than *Guilty Men*.

## Priestley

At this point it is necessary to examine some of the material that Baxendale and Pawling use to sustain their case. A key figure, they claim, was the novelist/playwright, J.B. Priestley, whom they describe as: ' ... the supreme articulator of the "People's War" narrative'.[7] We are told that Priestley 'damns' pre-war England.[8] We are also told that within his writings he argued that the war was not being fought by the traditional ruling class, but by the ordinary folk of industrial England, the ordinary folk who wanted no return to the miseries of pre-war society.[9] Baxendale and Pawling present a Priestley whose wartime writings focus on the hardships endured by the industrial working class in the immediate pre-war period. Furthermore, they argue Priestley presented the war as an event that must lead to fundamental changes within society, rather than preserve the existing social structure. An examination of Priestley's writings reveal that, rather like the Bible, one can find whatever one wants within their pages.

To support their claim about Priestley's view of the 1930s Baxendale and Pawling quote this passage from his 1941 pamphlet, *Out of the People*:

> Surely one reason why the twenty years between wars now seem a tragic farce, even here at home, is that during this period we did not change values but merely cheapened them. It will be remembered as the era of nightclub haunting princes and gossip-writing peers. The masquerade still went on, though now the costumes were tattered and the masks rotting. No visitor to Britain seeing the ruined cotton mills and rotting shipyards of the North, the jerry-built bungalows and gimcrack factories of the South, exclaimed in wonder, as men had done once, at the virility, splendour and potent magic of our island life. How much was there here worth preserving .... The nation's mind was elsewhere, withdrawn, more than half asleep, charmed and lulled by politicians with a good bedside manner.[10]

Baxendale and Pawling greatly strengthen their case by their editing of this passage. Between the word 'rotting', at the end of the third sentence, and the sentence beginning 'No visitor to Britain', there are eleven lengthy sentences, which include the following passage:

> Meanwhile the last traces were vanishing of that older Britain whose hazy loveliness was recorded by Turner and Constable, Girtin and Cotman, whose wealth of character enriched the pages of Fielding and Sterne, Scott and Dickens, whose love and pain and ecstasy were made immortal by her lyric poets. Among these vanishing traces which give a special savour to this island, were quaint customs and quirks of local thought and feeling, quiet forgotten corners and immemorial traditions. It was nothing of this that the Conservatives succeeded in conserving, but only the secret of how to make money and retain power. This older Britain had to go, but what took its place had no like value, no new salt and savour; and no visitor to Britain seeing ....[11]

The first, minor, point to make about this is that Baxendale and Pawling have turned the 'n' in no visitor to Britain into a capital letter, that is they have made it the beginning of a sentence, which it clearly is not in the original. Second, it would seem from this passage that Priestley had an almost Churchillian feel for the timeless unities of British history. His attack on the Conservatives of the inter-war years, contained here, is based on the contention that they have failed to conserve an older, more worthwhile, largely rural, Britain. Indeed the tone of this passage is very similar to that of the brief remarks that the socially-conservative historian, G.M. Trevelyan, made on the twentieth century at the end of his *English Social History*:

> under the new conditions England bade fair to become one huge unplanned suburb. Motor traction created the urgent need for the state to control the development of the whole island, but unhappily the matter was left to chance and the building exploiter.[12]

Trevelyan was definitely not a proponent of the 'People's War'. According to his biographer, David Cannadine, he regretted virtually every change that had occurred in Britain since 1914.[13] He was, however, an extremely popular writer. His *English Social History*, first published in England in 1944, went through two further impressions by July 1945, and continued in print until the early 1960s.

To return to Priestley, Baxendale and Pawling make a number of references to the *Postscript* broadcasts that he made between 5 June and 20

October 1940. These are presented as key components in the construction of a 'People's War' mythology. In his *Postscript* of 16 June Priestley described a night duty that he had performed with the Local Defence Volunteer (later Home Guard) unit in the village (in Southern England) that was his home. It contained the following:

> There we were, ploughman and parson, shepherd and clerk, turning out at night as our forefathers had done before us, to keep watch and ward over the sleeping English hills and fields and farmsteads. I've mentioned Thomas Hardy, whose centenary has just been celebrated. Don't you find in his tales and poems, often derived from the tales he listened to as a boy, a sense that Napoleon, with *his* threatened invasion by the Grand Army at Boulogne was only just around the corner? And I felt, out in the night on the hilltop, that the watch they kept then was only yesterday ....[14]

This sounds very much like an appeal to 'timeless unities': the rural setting, the invocation of Thomas Hardy, the connection between the dangers of 1940 and the threat posed by Napoleon, the use of archaic language ward and watch all, taken together, represent a celebration of a relatively distant, heroic, rural past. Indeed, one might ask what separates Priestley from the following passage:

> We who have seen the unloosed surge of Nazi fanaticism and the Panzers breaking down the dams of civilisation are better able than our immediate predecessors to understand what the generation of Pitt and Nelson had to resist.[15]

Both extracts clearly draw parallels between the Napoleonic wars and the Nazi threat, and draw inspiration from them. The difference is that the second extract comes from Arthur Bryant's *The Years of Endurance 1793–1802*, first published in 1942. Bryant, like his friend Trevelyan, was not a proponent of 'People's War'. He was a bestselling, conservative historian, very definitely Churchillian in outlook.

Within Priestley's writings it is possible to find a celebration of rural life and the distant past. Clearly he was as wedded to the romance of our islands story as Churchill himself. The dichotomy drawn between a 'Churchillian' perspective and a 'People's War' viewpoint seems, at least in the case of Priestley, questionable.

## The pamphlets

Another important component of the 'People's War' analysis, according to Baxendale and Pawling, was the series of yellow-jacketed pamphlets published during the war by Victor Gollancz. On the face of it these best-selling pamphlets do seem primarily concerned to assail the record of the Conservative-dominated governments of the inter-war period. *Guilty Men* (1940) attacked their record on re-armament; *The Trial of Mussolini* (1943) documented the close relationship between British Conservatives and the Italian fascist regime; *Your MP* (1944) was a critical analysis of Conservative voting patterns in the House of Commons, and so it goes on. However, the historiographical analysis contained in these pamphlets is more complex than it at first appears. There is within them a long perspective that implicitly characterises the inter-war years as an aberration from a natural line of historical development.

In *Your MP*, Tom Wintringham, when discussing Conservative neglect of Britain's merchant marine, makes the following point:

> our rulers were also people who had the chance to travel, to see far peoples and cities. Better than any of us, they should have realised what every previous ruling class of Britain had realised since Queen Elizabeth's days: that Britain lives by its seamen and its ships.[16]

The implication of this is that Wintringham, a former communist, is not attacking the British ruling class because he objected to such a body per se, rather he is attacking them because, in an historical perspective, they have proved to be an inadequate ruling class. Michael Foot's *Guilty Men* has a similar orientation; speaking of those politicians who ruled Britain between the wars the pamphlet states:

> They found us at the end of a great war, wounded indeed and weary, but victorious, confident of solving our manifold problems and capable of doing so. MacDonald and Baldwin took over a great empire, supreme in arms and secure in liberty. They conducted it to the edge of national annihilation.[17]

Again, within this extract the short-term perspective is linked to a longer term view. Up until 1918, the extract suggests, the trajectory of British history was following the right course, a great empire had been created and the First World War won. All of this was betrayed by inadequate politicians.

Aneurin Bevan also balanced a long-term with a short-term perspective. His 1944 pamphlet, *Why Not Trust the Tories?* analyses the betrayal of the promises made at the end of the First World War. In his concluding chapter Bevan cites the seventeenth century Putney debates to argue that the coming General Election represented the point to which British history had been moving for the last 300 years; the point at which the population could curb the powers of the propertied by the exercise of their democratic rights.[18] Within such a long view, again the inter-war period can be seen as a minor interruption.

In his 1943 pamphlet, *The Trial of Mussolini*, Michael Foot argued that British Labour represented the twentieth-century version of Gladstonian-Liberal internationalism; a political tradition that supported national-democratic movements throughout Europe in the nineteenth century. It was, he argued, the abandonment of this policy by the Conservatives that so damaged Britain in the inter-war period. An electoral victory for Labour would, in his view, lead to the restoration of the foreign policy of the nineteenth century.[19]

It is not possible, in the light of the above, to argue that these pamphlets focus solely on the inter-war period. The points they make about the recent past are clearly located within a longer term historical perspective, a perspective that represented the 1920s and 1930s as a deviation from the overall line of historical development. The generally positive view of the pre-1918 period means that these pamphlets do not condemn capitalism as such, but rather they focus on the inadequacies of individual politicians. This meant that the distance between a progressive Conservative, like Quintin Hogg, and the Gollancz pamphleteers is actually quite small. Hogg argued that the politicians of the inter-war period were inadequate but not malicious, whereas Foot argued that they were inadequate and malicious. Hogg argued that a new international order was needed for the post-war world, so too did Konni Zilliacus, in the 1945 pamphlet, *Can the Tories Win the Peace?* Of course they disagreed about which political party could best achieve this end, but this could simply be seen as the product of an adversarial political system, rather than of fundamental historiographical differences.

## A common stock of references

What all of this amounts is the conclusion that Baxendale and Pawling's analysis is, at the very least, unproven. Labour's victory in 1945 hardly provides conclusive evidence of the dominance of a 'People's War' discourse.

Labour won the election, but only took 47.8 per cent of the total vote. Furthermore the cinematic evidence which could, through its relationship to the market, be argued to closely reflect popular attitudes demonstrates the popularity, in the form of war films, of deeply conservative discourses.

The examination of the Gollancz pamphlets and the Priestley material also suggests that the dichotomy outlined by Baxendale and Pawling is much too sharply drawn. All of the writers cited by them as representing the 'People's War' viewpoint, as they define it, locate their analyses of the 1930s within a long-term historical perspective. The Gollancz pamphleteers do venerate the more distant past, indeed a great deal of the venom they direct at the Conservatives is inspired by their belief that they had abandoned and betrayed earlier traditions and policies. In the case of Priestley, one can demonstrate the existence of a veneration of the rural past that is, in Baxendale and Pawling's terms, 'Churchillian'.

The criticisms of Priestley, Foot, *et al.* all focus upon the inter-war period as a departure from the previously positive trajectory of British politics and society. There is no real criticism of capitalism as such, indeed, it can be demonstrated that the Second World War witnessed the final abandonment, by the Labour Left, of anything resembling Marxism. Consequently, it can also be argued that the very limited nature of the Left's analysis is the reason for the relatively weak resonance that the 1930s carries with the population at large today. After the war Baxendale and Pawling can only demonstrate the negative view of the 1930s by reference to the work of professional historians and political activists, not, that is, to the general population. Indeed, Labour lost office in 1951, only seven years after the end of the war, and did not regain it until 1964. This record hardly seems to indicate the persistence of a deeply felt popular reaction to the negative experiences of the 1930s.

In the 1990s Will Hutton, often regarded as a New Labour ideologue, praised the economic policies of the Conservative-dominated National Government of the 1930s in his best-selling book, *The State We're In*.[20] Jarrow may have been murdered by such policies[21] but today New Labour rehabilitates the killer and forgets the victim, and nobody seems to notice.

To understand the nature of the material produced by the group identified by Baxendale and Pawling as representing the 'People's War' point of view, it is important to remember that many of them were on a rightward political trajectory. Until at least 1937 the Labour Left, including Bevan and Foot, had rejected re-armament on the basis that this would put arms into the hands of their class enemies. During the course of the war they abandoned class-based politics for a form of radical patriotism. This alone meant that in relative terms such figures were moving closer to their Conservative opponents. Within their rhetoric Priestley, Foot and the others combined appeals for a better tomorrow with reference to the distant historical past. The approach is perfectly encapsulated in an extract from Humphrey Jennings's 1941 film, *Words for Battle*. The clip opens with a shot of evacuees, labelled and ready for departure, it then cuts to a shot of an LCC plaque, indicating a house occupied at one time by William Blake. At this point Laurence Olivier begins to read the second verse of *Jerusalem*. We see a steam train passing through the terraces of the city, then, as Olivier reaches the line: 'Till we have built Jerusalem'. the scene changes to shots in rural settings, children are shown boating, fishing, running through sunlit woods. Here, then we have a reference to the past in the form of the poet Blake, a reference that simultaneously provides a vision of the future: 'Jerusalem, in England's green and pleasant land.' It is a vision of the future as a return to the rural past.

Rather than there being two clearly distinct popular historiographic traditions developing during the course of the Second World War, there seems to be a generalised appeal to British history within which figures nominally from the Right and Left drew on a common stock of images and references. There were clearly differences of emphasis, but these were not sufficiently marked to justify the analysis of Baxendale and Pawling. The consequence of this process is that the 1930s appear to survive in popular memory not as a continuing stimulus for class indignation, but through the rosy glow of nostalgic bread advertisements, reified historical 'experiences', of the Wigan Pier variety and television costume dramas.

## Notes

1. John Baxendale, Christopher Pawling, *Narrating the Thirties: A decade in the making: 1930 to the present* (Macmillan, 1996), p.2.
2. Ibid., p.128.
3. Ibid., p.137.
4. George Orwell expressed similar views about British national charateristics, see George Orwell, *The Lion and the Unicorn* (1940) in Sonia Orwell, Ian Angus (eds), *The Collected Essays and Journalism and Letters of George Orwell, Vol.2, My Country Right or Left* (Penguin, 1977), pp.79–81.
5. Quintin Hogg, *The Left Was Never Right* (Faber and Faber, 1945), p.214.
6. Ibid., p.216.
7. Baxendale and Pawling, op cit., p.134.
8. Ibid., p.135.
9. Ibid., p.136.

10. Ibid., pp.135–6.
11. J.B. Priestley, *Out of the People* (Collins, 1941), pp.105–6.
12. G.M. Trevelyan, *English Social History* (Reprint Society, 1948), p.591.
13. David Cannadine, *G.M. Trevelyan: A life in history* (Fontana, 1993), p.57.
14. J.B. Priestley, *Postscripts* (Heinemann, 1940), p.12.
15. Arthur Bryant, *The Years of Endurance 1793–1802* (Fontana, 1961), p.12.
16. Tom Wintringham, *Your MP* (Gollancz, 1944), p.83.
17. Michael Foot, Peter Howard, Frank Owen, *Guilty Men* (Gollancz 1940), p.19.
18. Aneurin Bevan, *Why Not Trust the Tories?* (Gollancz), p.88.
19. Michael Foot, *The Trial of Mussolini* (Gollancz, 1943), p.81.
20. Will Hutton, *The State We're In* (Jonathan Cape, 1995), pp.125–8.
21. Ellen Wilkinson, *The Town That Was Murdered* (LBC, 1939).

# Reviews

## Culture and imperialism

Keith Ansell Pearson, Benita Parry and Judith Squires, *Cultural Readings of Imperialism: Edward Said and the gravity of history* (Lawrence and Wishart, London, 1997), ISBN 0-853-1584-0, £14.99.

Edward Said has profoundly influenced our world as a political activist and as committed intellectual. The publication of his *Orientalism* twenty years ago will most likely prove to be his most influential contribution not withstanding his tireless advocacy of the rights of the Palestinians. *Orientalism* and later *Culture and Imperialism* have changed the terms of the discussion about the character of the West and its relations with the world beyond. His work has had an impact on literary criticism, the margins of Middle Eastern studies and has been a foundational contribution to cultural studies. It is difficult to imagine what discussions of the West and the ex-colonial world would be like had Edward Said not written *Orientalism*. In their collection, Pearson, Parry and Squires bring together thirteen scholars who debate Said's work in the context of the 'gravity of history'. Said's *Orientalism* plots the construction of the Orient in English and French literature. In this he mobilizes the work of Michel Foucault to conclude that settled notions of the West as modern and rational as against the East as backward and irrational are encoded into a discourse which seeps into western consciousness and sustains colonial and postcolonial power. The authors of this collection are concerned lest the notion of discourse become detached from history.

The book takes the themes of identity, nationalism, colour and religion and re-works them sometimes in fascinating ways. Ella Shohat challenges our imagination in offering a relational analysis of Palestinians and Jews through referring to Columbus. The use of Columbus decentres the usual binary conflict analysis of Palestine and Israel. Robert Bernaconi poses some difficult questions about the origins of Greek philosophy while Kadiatu Kanneh raises the European genocidal view of Africa. These and the other contributors are largely drawn from scholars working in the fields of English literature, cultural studies and women's studies. This reflects the fact that Said's work has had little impact on the social sciences or indeed on the theory of the Left. It is left to Robert Young to raise this pertinent issue. In all the work which has developed out of *Orientalism*, the charting of the collusion of Western academic knowledge with the history and ideology of European colonialism remains relatively neglected. (p.127)

Young is being somewhat modest and he is one of the few who has made a significant contribution in his *Colonial Desire: Hybridity in Theory, Culture and Race* (Routledge, 1995). His book is chilling as it marshals the evidence that European racism is not the product of the ignorant masses, but the result of scholarly endeavours. The universities of the nineteenth century became the citadels of a Darwinism which attempted to prove that not only was the West economically and socially advanced but that European man was at the top of the evolutionary tree. The measuring of heads, the length of noses, the size of lips, the curl of hair were not cruelties thought up by the Nazis or the apartheid regimes but rather reported in scientific journals and books. Young is quite correct that the painful task of re-reading the west's history has not been completed. It is this which makes the notion of the gravity of history — some outside material force — difficult to come to grips with. History remains a narrative which like literature encodes the values of power.

Young's piece also touches on the thorny issue of Marxist approaches to colonialism and indeed to race. He quotes Engels's view that the one of the problems of the English working class is the way in which 'assimilates a great part of Irish characteristics.' Engels's use of the term 'Irish filth' is startling. But then so is Marx's opposition to the Indian rising (see Bhikhu Parekh' chapter, p.190). Indeed Marx and Engels and the subsequent Marxist and socialist movements were deeply connected to the Western narrative and in the confidence that the west represented progress and modernity. This above all perhaps underlines Young's contention. It was not only in the universities that racism was being developed as an academic science, but working-class movement itself was deeply embedded in racist and colonialist attitudes. Marx's use of racist abuse against Ferdinand Lassalle is a symptom of a wider issue. Marx's racist language — derogatory remarks about Jews and Blacks — was not an individual outpouring, but connected to his Western view of history. For Marx the Indian uprising of 1857 was no more progressive than the resistance of first nation Americans against the European settlers. In the triumph of European colonialism — including its genocide — Marx saw the progress of Capital and with it the creation a working class that would put an end to it. To the victim of colonialism there was not much to choose between Marx's progress and the Imperialist conquest. Both represented Europe's power to destroy cultures and languages, introduce forms of slavery, and in the America's and Australaisa, genocide. For these peoples there is little in Marx's talk of creating the material conditions for human liberation that contains much attraction. Human liberation appears more as European power built on their graves. In the ex-colonial world from Australia to northern Canada this is still a critical issue.

Marx like many nineteenth-century intellectuals assumed a relationship between Europe and progress. He even went so far as to typify the lowest form of the mode of production as 'Asiatic' which appears at odds with the notion that recorded history is the history of class struggles. Marx and Engels also relied upon the theory of oriental despotism when analyzing non-Western societies. Trotsky was to turn to that very term to denounce the Stalinist regime.

Pearson, Parry and Squires have performed an important service in producing a collection which should provoke much thought amongst social scientists and theoreticians on the Left. The one weakness of the book is that the question of history is not itself satisfactorily addressed. History is much referred to but we are never sure whether it is merely a construction or a material reality. This has great significance as the texts of the social sciences and of the Left are encoded with the Western view of history and its appropriation of progress and modernity. Much work needs to be done in re-reading these academic and political texts and in reconstructing a social and political theory that can empower our multicultural world. This project must aim at an inclusive theory and practice in which no one culture has a privileged place. Said has, above all, taught us that we have to liberate western theory from its own colonial occupation if it is to contribute to a genuine universalism.

*John Strawson*

# The Challenges of Postmodernism

**John Belchem and Neville Kirk** (eds), *Languages of Labour* (Ashgate Publishing, Aldershot, 1997), ISBN 1-85928-428-0, viii + 222pp., £40.00 hbk
**Ellen Meiksins Wood and John Bellamy Foster** (eds), *In Defense of History: Marxism and the postmodern agenda* (Monthly Review Press, New York, USA, 1997), ISBN 0-8534-5983-5, 204pp., £13.95 pbk. Distributed in Britain by Zed Books, London.

The editors of *Languages of Labour* aim to show how analyses of language can contribute to understanding in labour history. But they have a wider argument. Their overall objective is to throw into relief the ways that the 'linguistic turn' promoted by some postmodernist writers involves 'despairing and unproductive fragmentation and relativism ... narrow textual range' and 'literal and anti-realist readings'.

There is no doubt that the book achieves its more limited aim. *Languages of Labour* proves that there 'currently exist continuing and vital areas of interest and debate concerning language and identity within 'modernist' labour and social history'. Melanie Tebbutt's chapter, for example, analyses 'workplace gossip' as central to a 'finely nuanced, micro-study of the complex nature of ... "worker consciousness"'.[1] And Karen Hunt shows how the language of the Social Democratic Federation's 'socialism appeared to be universalistic, but at its root it was fractured. At its heart was a theory which overstamped class interests on to any other identities so that the apparently gender-neutral terms and concepts ... always turned out to reflect the experiences of white working class males'. A total of seven chapters focus on the use of language in particular contexts and struggles which will be of interest to readers of this journal.

It is more debateable whether *Languages of Labour* illustrates that '"modernist" labour and social history' is really engaging with the challenges of postmodernism, and convincingly addressing those challenges. This is partly because Kirk and Belchem sometimes let show a defensive tendency to caricature 'postmodernism', suggesting that postmodernists never contextualise language, whereas the labour historians published here do. By defining all postmodernists together with those few extremists who entirely reject 'realism's epistemological and methodological credentials and procedures' in favour of seeing 'nothing beyond subjectivity', the editors seem tempted to make it easy for themselves to see off the challenge.

The book's central anti-postmodernist arguments are developed in Richard Price's theoretical chapter. He sees 'British social history' as a crucial field of engagement for postmodernism' because of its particularly successful combination of the empirical method and Marxist theory. Early on, he acknowledges that 'postmodernism plays a useful role, if only in causing us to re-examine our epistemologies' and 'in reminding us to beware of claims to absolute or universal truth'. But Price soon moves on from such notes of guarded approval to develop sustained polemics. He scores many direct hits, as when he exposes postmodernists' tendency to caricature all modernist and positivist traditions as attempts at the crude totalisation of knowledge. Postmodernism thus fails 'to pay due attention to the space within the Enlightenment tradition for ambiguity, contradiction, and pluralistic instability of meaning'.

Price's chapter, like the editors' introduction, itself contains an instability of meaning about what postmodernism is. When Price is in full critical flight, and when Kirk and Belchem are being most hostile, they seem to cast 'postmodernism' as a unified and coherent set of beliefs which can be straightforwardly targeted. At less intense moments in their texts, though, there is recognition that 'postmodernism is more a field of debate than anything else' and that it 'is best understood as a collection of intellectual postures towards representation and meaning'. Such observations mean that, overall, Price and the editors cannot be judged guilty of one-sidedness or weak polemic. Kirk and Belchem further point out that some of their book's (female) contributors 'recognise the important ... influence of the postmodernist "turn" — in focusing attention of the partial gender blindness of "traditional", labour history'. And they acknowledge that distinctions must be made between different 'postmodernists', citing for example the judgement of Eileen Yeo and Ali Rattansi that Foucault's notion of discourse is socially situated and is not 'free floating referential or fully autonomous'.

What is being perhaps being suggested at such points is that we can make a distinction between a 'strong' postmodernism, which tends to deny the possibility of our making sense of the world, and 'weak' postmodernisms, insights and cautions from which we should admit so as to help us better make sense of the world.

This point is suggested in Richard J. Evans's conclusion to his recent thoughtful, balanced engagement with postmodernist challenges to 'established' methods of historical investigation. Evans's judgement is that 'despite all the various pronouncements of its demise by postmodernists, social history is not dead. Undeniably, it has lost, or is in the course of abandoning, its universalising claim to be the key to the whole of historical understanding. To this extent, the postmodernist critique has been not only successful but also liberating. By directing historians' attention to language, culture and ideas, it has helped free them to develop more complex models of causation and to take seriously subjects they may have neglected before'.[2]

Evans's excellent book should not be confused with the similarly-titled collection from the Monthly Review Press in New York. Key contributions to *In Defense of History* tend towards the defensive insistence in the face of the challenges of postmodernism that Marxism is still right. Ellen Meiksins Wood suggests that postmodernism is just another of the reactionary denials of the possibility of progress that the Left has had to see off before. Her polemic against 'strong' postmodernism admits no validity in any of the criticisms made of Marxism from postmodern standpoints.

Arguing that 'we are living in a historical moment that more than any other demands a universalistic project' and 'that this is just the right time to revitalize Marxist critique', she spells out that the editorial aim in this book has been to re-state an already existing 'historical materialism' against the new enemy. When contributions were invited, it was stressed that the intention was not 'that people like us should abandon our terrain. On the contrary, part of the object is to demonstrate that our terrain is where it's at — for example, that the old bread-and-butter issues of the Left ... are still at the centre of things'.

Not all contributions to *In Defense of History* are wearily predictable. Terry Eagleton makes some telling points wittily in 'where do postmodernists come from?' He convincingly locates an origin of the postmodern impulse in an emphatic defeat suffered by the Left, not so much through the collapse of communism as in Left responses to the '"successes" of capitalism'. But naming this source of postmodernism does not mean that it does not have to do with something real — the defeat and disorientation which Eagleton sees is not undone by claiming that it is merely the result of an unnecessary intellectual choice in the face of material circumstances.

There are stimulating points, too, in Mulhearn's brief survey of the field of cultural studies, which, he argues, has collapsed politics into culture and has thus served as one of the slippery slopes down which many of 'the intellectual Left' have slid into postmodernism. And there are some thoroughly convincing passages in the book, such as Fredric Jameson's succinct 'five theses on actually existing Marxism'. This piece strikes a different tone from most others in the book by identifying 'that which has been labelled by some as postmodernity' as having to do with real expressions of the specific ways in which capitalism is currently changing and operating.

But most contributions to *In Defense of History* are frustratingly closed pieces in which Marxists refuse to admit any flaws in the 'ism' they long ago dedicated themselves to. Attempting to sustain this position in the context of a consideration of postmodernism, some end up being very dogmatic and one-sided. For all the clever elegance of his writing, Kenan Malik's contribution on race is a crude piece, conflating the relativist excesses of strong postmodernism with any recognition of the value of particularism, and suggesting that the only basis for strategies against oppression is a universalism which tends to deny the specificities of those particular identities on the basis of which, in fact, many people organise in a progressive way.

Such apparently 'rational' arguments seem n fact to be based on an emotional flight to apparent certainties in the face of the radical questions raised by postmodernism. In his 'Languages of Labour' chapter, Price pinpoints those consequences of 'strong' postmodernism which often provoke inpatient knee-jerk dismissal by those schooled in rationalist discourses such as Marxism: it 'leads inevitably to a total relativism' ... 'the postmodernist abandonment of reason' opens 'the way to political nihilism'.

But those who are not political nihilists, and in fact are working to develop projects such as socialism and movements against oppression, should not be too quick to dismiss the real challenges of postmodernism. To some degree, they should be welcomed and allowed to interrogate modernist and rationalist mindsets such as Marxism and social science, so that, as Richard Evans suggests, these disciplines and their capacity to change as well as to explain the world night be strengthened from the engagement with postmodernism.

For this reason, it is pleasing to see the issues which are the focus of *Languages of Labour* continuing to be debated and developed seriously. The May 1997 conference of the Society for the Study of Labour History in Manchester was a stimulating event, bringing together alleged postmodernists such as Patrick Joyce with Kirk and Belchem and their co-thinkers. For all the awkwardness and failures of communication apparent in the sessions, this pro-active effort by the SSLH to engage properly with postmodern challenges has led to ongoing dialogue, with Patrick Joyce's paper appearing in *Labour History Review*, and John Belchem writing very sensitively on the reconstruction of labour history in the context of 'the postmodern mood'.[3] His recent conclusion on the tasks ahead needs to be taken as a compass for those working in the field. 'Labour history should not dismiss postmodernism. Its theoretical pretensions (and obfuscatory prose) should be resisted, but its focus and practice — less novel and innovatory than its practitioners claim — should be embraced within the widening agenda of labour history.'[4]

*Mike Waite*
*Mike Waite is book reviews editor of* Socialist History

## Notes

1. Tebbutt's book *Women Talk? A Social History of 'Gossip' in Working Class Neighbourhoods 1880–1960* has previously been positively discussed in *Socialist History*. See Karen Triggs's review in issue 8, 1995, pp.101–3.
2. *In Defence of History* (London, 1997), pp.183–4.
3. Patrick Joyce, 'Refabricating labour history; or, from the labour history to the history of labour', in *Labour History Review*, SSLH/Edinburgh University Press, vol.62, no.2, summer 1997, p.147–52.
4. John Belchem, 'Reconstructing labour history', in *Labour History Review*, SSLH/Edinburgh University Press, vol.62 no.3, winter 1997, pp.318–23.

# Communist Historiography

**Richard Pipes (ed.)**, *The Unknown Lenin: From the secret archive* (Yale University Press, New Haven and London, 1996), ISBN 0-300-06919-7, £18.50 pbk; **Neil Harding**, *Leninism* (Macmillan, Basingstoke and London, 1996), ISBN 0-333-66482-5, £45.00, hbk, 0-333-66483-3, £14.99 pbk.

The opening up of hitherto closed Moscow archives in recent years has revealed that the 55 Russian volumes of *Lenin's Complete Collected Works* are not complete at all 3714 Lenin documents, which were not included, have now become accessible. Some of them have in the 1990s been published in Russian journals.

It is a selection of 113 of these archive documents, of varying lengths, that the first of these books makes available to English-language readers. Its editor, Richard Pipes, was Reagan's director of East European and Soviet Affairs for the National Security Council. He sees these writings as confirmation of his longstanding condemnation of Lenin as the founder of the 'evil empire' — 'a heartless cynic, who in many ways provided a model for Stalin'. These are all documents which the Soviet authorities kept in a secret archive because they feared that they would be seen to reflect unfavourably on their official sanitised model of the humanist Lenin.

Students of Soviet history, who have for some years been able to take stock of this and/or similar material, will not find much in Pipes's book to lead them to modify their present views on Lenin. Others, however, exposed to such documents for the first time, will find not a little in it which is disturbing and may call for reassessments. This will particularly be the case with its uncovering of an unacceptably authoritarian and at times brutal streak in the Bolshevik leader. This manifested itself notably when he was leading the Soviet state under the strains of the civil war and the ensuing famine, Thus, for example, we find him in August 1918 giving instructions for the hanging in Penza of 'no fewer than one hundred known kulaks, rich men, bloodsuckers'; in August 1919 threatening to 'exterminate every Cossack to a man' in Guriev; and in the same month insisting on 'merciless arrests among the strikers' in a printworkers' strike. In March 1922 he was demanding that the Party's Political Bureau give the judicial authorities a detailed directive for a trial of as many representatives of the local clergy and middle class as possible in Shuia and the 'execution by firing squad of a very large number of the most Influential and dangerous Black Hundreds' in that city as well as in Moscow and other clerical centres.

Documents to be found in this volume do not always bear out Pipes's interpretation of them. He asserts that a letter from Lenin to the Old Bolshevik Berzin in August 1919 provides the missing proof that the leader of the October Revolution was 'a German agent in the strict meaning of the word.' In fact Lenin's statement in it that some unspecified 'Berliners will send some money' to help produce pro-Bolshevik international propaganda material is far from supporting such a claim. Nor is there anything in Lenin's report to the Ninth Party Conference in September 1920 to warrant Pipes's assertion that this reveals that the Red Army's counter-offensive into ethnic Poland 'was not merely to sovietise Poland but to use it as a springboard for the invasion of Germany and England.' Pipes' talk of Lenin's 'utter disregard for human life' is hardly confirmed by his statement in the same report that a winter campaign against the Poles must be avoided 'because for us the lives of ten thousand Russian workers and peasants are of far greater value than anything else.'

Apologetics for Lenin are certainly not called for. However to base one's overall estimate of him on his most discreditable utterances as selected and interpreted by Pipes in this book would be grossly unfair and onesided.

Neil Harding's book, based on a deep study of Lenin's writings throughout his life, provides a balance and perspective lacking in Pipes's muck-raking compilation. Whereas Pipes presents Lenin as an unprincipled, power-seeking opportunist — 'first and foremost a tactician who modified his opinions to fit the situation in hand' — Harding insists that from the

1914–17 period 'a more or less integrated and consistent body of ideas did inform Lenin's actions.' At the heart of this was Lenin's analysis of imperialism as an entirely new epoch in history. By throwing humanity into a senseless slaughter in the First World War, it put on the international agenda the overthrow of capitalism and the advent of socialism. He shows that it was against this theoretical background that Lenin conceived and justified the Bolshevik-led October Revolution. Although because of its backwardness Russia was not yet ready for the introduction of socialism, he believed that the establishment of Soviet power there would help spark off socialist revolutions in developed capitalist countries.

Unlike Pipes, who dismisses the October Revolution as a simple *'coup d'état'*, Harding recognises the contradictory elements in it. On the one hand, it reflected a momentous shift in popular opinion against the Kerensky government and the war. On the other, there were 'elements of Blanquism' in the way the Bolshevik leadership organised and timed the October insurrection in Petrograd in such a way as to present the democratically elected Second Congress of Soviets with a fait accompli.

Harding shows that when Lenin and the Bolsheviks came to power they were genuinely committed to the establishment of a democratic 'commune state' with its emphasis on a radical transformation of the relations of domination and subordination characteristic of class-divided societies. The realisation of this perspective was however dependent on the expected spread of the world revolution. Finding itself isolated and invaded, Harding believes that any political regime in Russia would have had to resort to authoritarian measures. What he blames Lenin and his colleagues for is attempting to make a virtue out of a necessity by dramatically redefining socialism. It was no longer presented as re-shaping power relations and 'putting an end to being bossed', but in terms of transforming productive relations and maximising output. A small number of Communists established a political monopoly. 'In the absence of public support [this] led, ineluctably, to state coercion and terror,' representing a 'fundamental change of stance' from the original Bolshevik intentions when they took power. Although Harding sees 'a large measure of heroism' in Lenin's deathbed struggle against Stalin, he concludes with some exaggeration that up till that time he was 'complicit in all that made Stalin and Stalinism possible'.

Harding rightly insists that Marxism was Lenin's intellectual inspiration and reference point, arguing more controversially that 'Leninism was authentic Marxism'. He goes too far, in this reviewer's opinion, in arguing that elitist and anti-democratic elements in Leninism have their roots in the 'beguiling certainties' of Marx's 'philosophical scheme'. It was, after all,

Marx, who gave as his favourite motto 'De omnibus dubitandum' (it is necessary to have doubts about everything)!

A very useful feature of Neil Harding's well researched and thought-provoking book is a *Chronology of Events* and a guide to the 45 volumes of *Lenin's Collected Works in English*.

*Monty Johnstone*
*A member of the Socialist History Society, he has written extensively on communist history*


**Noreen Branson**, *History of the Communist Party of Great Britain, 1941–1951* (Lawrence and Wishart, London, 1997), ISBN 0-85315-862-2, viii + 262pp, £14.99 pbk.

This is the fourth part of the official history of the Communist Party of Great Britain (CPGB). The first two were written by James Klugman in the 1960s. When the project began, the forward march of labour seemed unhaltable. To Communists, social democracy appeared the main impediment to socialism, whilst Margaret Thatcher, if she registered at all, gave the impression of being a conventional Tory lady with a strange accent and even stranger hats. It was, then, a very different world from our own.

Given the CPGB's painful orthodoxy, allowing even the archloyalist Klugman to write the Party's history must have seemed rather risky to some. Hitherto, Communist historians had steered well clear of the history of Communism. Even the independently minded Christopher Hill, Eric Hobsbawm and Edward Thompson, had avoided writing about the period after 1917. However, fears that Klugman would pen anything other than an orthodox, uncritical — and boring — narrative of the Party's early years were misplaced. There would be no self-criticism at Central Committee meetings over his work.

On Klugman's death, Noreen Branson wrote the third volume, covering the years 1926–41; this was published in 1985. In this fourth part Branson takes the story to 1951: it consequently covers the period of the Party's greatest popularity, in terms of both numbers and ideas. The author researched the book during years which saw the triumph of Thatcherism, the CPGB's self-dissolution and the collapse of the Soviet Union. Capitalism, according to some intellectuals, had defeated socialism. This was, to say the least of it, an intriguing time to write about British Communism in the 1940s, especially given the new light in which many historians now view politics and popular culture.

Branson's object is 'to set the record straight'. Claiming that the aims and objectives of the Party have been 'much distorted by some historians' she simply wants to put the CPGB's side of the story. In so doing, she makes the familiar point that the Party, whilst 'never very large', enjoyed an influence much wider than its size would imply'. Her conclusion is that, whilst the Party was too uncritical of the Soviet Union, it had many positive achievements to its credit. Specifically, the CPGB defended the interests of working people, both male and female; supported the movement for colonial freedom; and opposed Britain's close relationship with the United States. More generally, despite the Cold War, Party members continued to 'spread the message' by advocating that capitalism be replaced by socialism to ensure 'a peaceful future, rising living standards, and a good life for all'.

Branson's book evokes, in its approach to the Party, those studies of the labour movement bureaucracy Henry Pelling and others wrote in the 1950s and 1960s. This is the history of the Party as organisation with all that entails. It is true that some areas are covered which earlier labour historians might have overlooked. In particular, there is a chapter on the Party's promotion of equality for women. Yet, despite this, Branson's is a resolutely old-fashioned approach to politics and the Party's relation to wider society.

Branson also cites a lot of facts. Thus, the numbers of Congress delegates are noted with careful precision; there is even an appendix which catalogues members of Executive Committees of the period. There is nothing wrong with this: I am sure such information is useful to some, as will be the extensive paraphrasing of speeches and documents. However, Branson devotes precious little time to analysing this information.

Perhaps that is just as well for, if antediluvian in method, Branson's attempt to 'set the record straight', means she is locked into a defensive, embattled mind-set that defined much of British Communism, especially in its later days. Consequently, she has produced a picture of the Party almost as distorted as those written by the unnamed historians with whom she so disagrees. Indeed, my suspicion is that much of her analysis would be familiar to readers of *Daily Worker* editorials of the later 1950s. Whilst this may persuade the naive or reinforce the prejudices of unreconstructed former CPGB members, it will make no converts amongst informed sceptics. One example of Branson's approach will have to suffice. Herbert Morrison's view that the Communist Party was subordinate to Moscow are dismissed as groundless. Branson even quotes Harry Pollitt during the Party's campaign to affiliate to Labour, to the effect that the CPGB was entirely financed by its members and not dependent upon the Soviet Union.

Honest Harry may have believed this to be the case: historians are now better informed about, if not Moscow Gold, then at least the Kremlin's cross-subsidy of King Street. Whilst some critics of the CPGB have, in the past, deliberately exaggerated the Party's subservience to Stalin, it is unforgivable for Branson to overlook such awkward knowledge. It was because of this attempt to delude oneself and others, albeit for 'honourable' reasons, that the likes of Edward Thompson left the Party in 1956. It is disappointing that such contortions are still performed, decades later, in a work which purports to be objective. In this way, Branson tells the reader more about the Party than she probably realised.

Whilst an accessible work, the history of the British Communist Party should not be judged on the basis of this book, nor those three volumes which preceded it. There are many now working on the Party who are less influenced by the Cold War's Manichean outlook and have already produced more sophisticated accounts. However, a question which bears constant repetition is: how much attention does an organisation whose official membership never exceeded 56,000 actually merit? One of the many annoying things about this book is its self-importance. Although the 1940s was the Party's most successful decade it, nonetheless, remained a marginal force. Branson and others would dispute this view, citing its work with squatters and the like, but it would have been useful if she had acknowledged and accounted for the limitations of the Party' s popular 'success'. Instead, one is confronted by sectarian condescension: quite how the Labour leadership managed to get so many things wrong and yet retain the support of millions I will never know — the British must have been very stupid. At the very least, then, Branson's work could have done with a little humility. Counter-factuals are fashionable these days: how different would Britain have been without the CPGB?

*Steven Fielding*
*Dept of Politics and Contemporary History, University of Salford*

**Margarita Tupitsyn**, *The Soviet Photograph, 1924–1937* (New Haven and London: Yale University Press, 1996), ISBN 0-3000-6450-0, x + 198pp., £27.50.

This handsome, lavishly illustrated volume brought back to me the excitement that Soviet posters and photomontages kindled in my generation in the two decades after the First World War.

Bright colours, bold marriage of images, breathtaking experiment with layout and typography, all gave fitting revolutionary form to the revolutionary messages expressed.

The aim, formulated by Lenin in 1921, was to 'link art and politics'. How to achieve that aim was then unclear, and became the focus of impassioned debate enduring until the mid-1930s.

The *avant-garde* artists who responded so enthusiastically to the October Revolution had, before 1917, developed an abstract visual language, but their views on the meaning and function of art remained closely linked to the sensibility of prerevolutionary modernism. Art that was devoid of overt subject matter or of figurative elements was seen as autonomous and beyond the concerns of everyday life. However, *avant-garde* photography and photomontage rapidly brought about a shift from advocacy of the autonomy of the work of art to assertion of its practical and political purpose. Photography was the catalyst in the last great experiment, in the search for the most effective ways to connect art, radical politics, and the peasant and proletarian masses.

In this pioneering history of *avant-garde* Soviet photography and photomontage between 1924 and 1937, Margarita Tupitsyn of Rutgers, the State University of New Jersey, analyses the function of the photographic image by reference, particularly, to the works of photographers such as Aleksandr Rodchenko, El Lissitzky, Gustav Klutsis, Valentina Kulagina, Sergei Sen'kin.

Thanks to perestroika, Tupitsyn had unprecedented access to the continuing Rodchenko/Stepanova studio, to the rich private archive of Gustav Klutsis, to the unpublished notes of Sergei Senikin, to the families of deceased photographers, and to the unequalled archives of *Sovetskoe foto*. From these and a wide range of other sources (such as Rodchenko's public lectures, Lissitzky's late writings on the mass media, and Kulagina's personal diaries) is distilled a vivid art history fashioned by impeccable scholarship, technical expertise, and keen political insight.

Tupitsyn cogently challenges the view that the Soviet avant garde 'peaked' in the 1920s and was subsequently forced to conform with 'Bolshevik politics'. She relates major examples of single-frame photography and photomontage to such events as the implementation of the New Economic Policy, the death of Lenin, Stalin's first and second Five-Year Plans, and to intensifying censorship of the arts. The writings of critics are shown to have been influential in the development of photography and photomontage during this dynamic period.

The unfamiliarity (to present-day scholars in East and West alike) of much of the abundant information and striking illustrations presented by Tupitsyn demands specially careful reading, as do the labyrinthine public controversies and in-group debates she so deftly and lucidly outlines. Nothing is taken for granted — as 'gospel truth'. One sees the once-maligned magazine USSR in Construction in a new light, and one turns to reconsider the currently fashionable strictures on socialist realism and its diverse modes of expression. The whole period is brightly illuminated.

Stimulating, beautifully written, and visually fascinating, this splendid book significantly advances our knowledge and understanding of an important, indefensibly neglected aspect of Russian art history and of its arcane political context.

*H.G.A. Hughes*

## Versailles and Modernity

**David Parker,** *Class and State in* Ancien Régime *France: The road to modernity* (Routledge, London, 1996), ISBN 0-4151-3647-4, xvii + 349pp., £40.00 hbk.

David Parker uses a form of Marxist historiography which takes account of recent lessons. Historical materialism is to be re-evaluated in the light of the collapse of the Berlin Wall, and the globalised market economy. It is none the worse for that. 'A central purpose of the book is to modify recent Marxist interpretations of the genesis, function and nature of absolute monarchy...'

Parker sees that by cracking the nut that is French absolutism, many other historical controversies can be solved, from the transition from feudalism to capitalism to the French revolution. This may seen an impossible task in a text of 280 pages, but through a judicious use of sources and a succinct prose style, he manages to convince most of the time. Although the book is centred on the French variant of absolutism which reached its apogee under Louis XIV, this is used as a pivot to examine other related themes.

The question in the book's title relates to the problematic nature of absolutism, French or otherwise. 'Historians and sociologists of every persuasion — whether Marxists, modernisers, structural functionalists, Whigs or just empirical observers — have all struggled to accommodate its hybrid, ambivalent and ambiguous features within their various conceptual frameworks' .

In his central chapters, Parker examines the seventeenth-century French economy, its politics and society, to argue that French absolutism was not an attempt at conversion from one mode of production to another, or an attempt to speed modernisation up, but that the connection between capitalism and absolutism is incidental, and that absolutism was an attempt by the French ruling class to impede the gathering momentum of modernisation. To this extent it was successful, but at a large cost.

The success of the *ancien régime* meant that the French economy became a good example of arrested development. The emergent markets of the sixteenth century were either stifled or completely eradicated by the demands of a state geared towards the preservation and extension of royal authority. An homogenous and nationwide market did not really exist — rather 'a number of regional ones and within these many local ones'. This is highlighted by the economic disparities between regions. Even areas within regions did not work in economic harmony — 'upper and lower Languedoc ... had virtually nothing in common'. This disparity could have led to much activity within and between regions, but this potential was hampered by a poor transport system, lack of a widespread merchant class and constant state intervention In terms of protectionism and regulatory measures. Indeed, the state has to take much of the blame for this poor situation. The policy of Mercantilism was devised not on the back of a strong market economy, but precisely because there was a lack of one.

The state's need for a centrally administered economy, due to military and fiscal demands, caused great distress amongst the peasantry and class conflict ensued. But any revolt had little chance of success as demographic stagnation due to war and plague wiped out many small property holders. This left a proletariat in the making, but without the resources to act either as a bulwark against the ruling class or as a generator of demand. Instead, landlords used this as an opportunity for further exploitation and an imposition of their will.

This imposition of control did not eradicate internal conflict, however, since the aristocracy were in an almost perpetual competition to maximise their own power, influence, status and share of wealth extracted from the labouring population. Potentially, this helped Louis XIV as any attempt by the different groupings within the aristocracy to unite in opposition to any centrally imposed edicts was bound to fail, due to mistrust and loathing. Instead they looked to the state for preferment.

It is therefore meaningless to talk of the different interests of the ruling class ... this is not surprising given that so much of the royal administration had literally been bought up by the seigneurial office holding élite, many of whom became enormously wealthy. 'If one was looking for a State apparatus which conformed to the vulgar Marxist notions of an instrument in the hands of the ruling class, it would be difficult to find a better example'.

Having said this, Parker quickly stresses that a vulgar Marxist reading of the period will by no means suffice. The nobility and the state itself has to be examined in ideological and cultural terms. Through the use of philosophical ideas such as 'the chain of being', the ruling class created a renewed sense of hierarchy and therefore created their own aristocratic identity out of the fractured society they saw about them.

The king was at the apex. Versailles was the epitome of the absolutist regime, acting as 'both court and government ... also the home of the very large royal family, whose concern over lineage and blood exemplified that of every noble line'. Versailles' very conservatism, its playing with rank, etiquette and privilege, was an embodiment of the social make up of France that the ruling class wanted to see. Louis played the part of tyrant, sun god, divine appointee and judge extremely well. It was a choice between this and the social dislocation of the previous hundred years leading up to the *Frondes*. The ruling class knew what they wanted and were willing to compromise some power and dignity in return for whatever largesse they could expropriate from the peasantry.

Parker's is a persuasive argument, addressing the problem of why the absolutist state appeared when it did in France. Perry Anderson's examination of absolutism as a mainly martial edifice relied heavily on East European examples, and looked less convincing when applied to Western Europe, especially France. Parker's use of Marxist theory in a convincing way should therefore be welcomed as an argument against those who would wish to see historical materialism consigned to the historical rubbish bin.

In the final chapter, Parker seems to overstretch himself. In fifty pages, he attempts to compare the different roads taken by France and England over two and a half centuries. France emerges as an example of arrested development. England, on the other hand, is shown to be an example of successful development. Britain was free of a supine bourgeoisie — by flexing its muscles against a series of weak kings in the seventeenth century it was able to achieve its aims.

If it didn't have a strong Left wing twist, this theme might read like something journalists such as Paul Johnson might warm to, with its suggestion that England's development was unproblematic whereas France's was impeded and slow. But 1789 hangs over the final segment of the book, a spectre of what is to come.

This over-ambitious final chapter is the only problematic part of an otherwise very readable and impressive book. It is an attempt at 'total history', studying a period from a Marxist viewpoint in a way which implies that state-centred ideologies will fail and should fail, whether they be French absolutism descending into the *ancien régime*, or the monolith of Stalinism which existed in Eastern Europe during the twentieth century.

*Donald Lowndes Sanderson*
*Donald Lowndes Sanderson is a secondary school teacher of history in south Yorkshire*

## Experiments with Extremes

**Momme Brodersen**, *Walter Benjamin: A biography* (London, Verso, 1996), ISBN 1-8598-4967-9, xvi + 334pp., £25.00 hbk.

In his essay 'The Storyteller' Benjamin reflected on how that once most public and indeed exemplary of events in an individual's life, death, has increasingly been severed and distanced from our existence. Death is no longer at the centre of our culture but takes place in hospitals and sanatoria without directly impinging upon the everyday lives of the living. For Benjamin, however, 'a man's knowledge or wisdom, but above all his real life — and this is the stuff that stories are made of — first assumes transmissible form at the moment of his death'. The moment of death retrospectively reorders everything that went before it and gives meaning and coherence to an individual life story. Death sanctions everything a storyteller can tell, it is the ultimate authority behind the narrative. Not surprisingly, therefore, the tragic circumstances of Benjamin's own death (apparently by suicide at the Franco-Spanish border in 1940, fleeing from the Nazis) has come to overshadow and sanction so many readings of his own life and work and perpetuate the popular image of a solitary, isolated and melancholic intellectual. It is one of the many pleasures of Momme Brodersen's eloquently written biography then to find restored to us a complex and contradictory thinker intensively engaged with the world around him.

From his early involvement with educational reform, through the German Youth Movement, to his final, if idiosyncratic, embracing of historical materialism Brodersen presents us with an image of Benjamin wrestling not just with esoteric questions of philosophy, aesthetics and theology but also with concrete social and political issues. Drawing extensively on Benjamin's letters and diaries, as well as his published manuscripts and journalism, the 'eloquent silence', which at various times throughout his life Benjamin was forced to present to the world, stands counterposed to the polemical and combative tone of so much of his writing.

Brodersen admirably treads the difficult path all biographers face of drawing out the continuities within a life and at the same time assessing those moments of discontinuity and rupture, when everything that preceded it is ordered anew. Benjamin's lifelong engagement with Judaism, for example, is evident in the posthumously published theses on history, just as his early preoccupation with Baudelaire prefigured the later Arcades project. But these later works are radically different in tone from the metaphysical and élitist concerns of his early writing, and Benjamin was quite consciously seeking a new form and style of writing to adequately express his new and revolutionary ideas. In the same year (1928) Benjamin published his most 'scholarly' text, *The Origin of German Tragic Drama*, he also published *One-Way Street*, a fragmentary and aphoristic text in which he sought to give 'a political exposition of (the development of) his own thoughts' — in a manner that 'experiments with extremes' and 'is not masked in the old-fashioned way'. Brodersen astutely and judiciously analyses the developments and divergences between Benjamin's early bourgeois elitism and esotericism and the later more overtly political writings. Benjamin's mysticism, for example, was never fully integrated or subsumed by his adherence to Marxism but this is no reason, as his more liberal advocates would have us accept, to privilege the theological over political. As with Benjamin's conception of the dialectical image, we find within this conjuncture of mysticism and materialism a yoking together of opposites in order to produce something radically and disturbingly new. Benjamin's 'conversion' to communism, then, cannot be dismissed as Popular Front bandwagon hopping, and which by implication he would have moved beyond had he survived, but rather as an attempt to resolve issues that could not be resolved within the limits of either German idealist philosophy or theology. What emerges from this biography is the sense of a thinker and writer constantly struggling with the limits of his own understanding.

The fragmentary and aphoristic nature of many of Benjamin's texts have also bestowed upon him something of the status of a postmodernist *avant la lettre*. And reading some of these early passages on language and representation, especially his reflections on the failure of language to fully represent reality and our need to conceive of writing in terms of its 'effects', one is struck by the contemporary resonance of these views. Indeed, in an almost Baudrillardian flourish, Benjamin writes that knowledge can determine action only by virtue of its linguistic structure, and such knowledge 'leads to silence'. Just as for Baudrillard today, the silence of the majority is seen as the ultimate act of resistance, silence for Benjamin 'was an expression of inner protest at contemporary events.' Such readings, however, are partial and superficial. Benjamin's reflections on the silence at the core of language, as Brodersen shows, must be seen in relation to Benjamin's specific historical situation and is hardly comparable with an apolitical postmodern quietism. Contemporary theories of discourse can only be extrapolated from Benjamin's enduring concern with questions of language and methodology if one sheds his early mystical kernel or later socio-linguistic concerns. Benjamin's antipathy to writing in a traditional academic style also chimes with certain tendencies within post-structuralism but again this experimentation with form took place within the context of a politically charged and revolutionary modernism and cannot be reduced to postmodern textuality. Perhaps the real test of any successful biography is that it leaves one with the desire to return to the work of the subject. Brodersen's intelligent and illuminating work left me with a sense that in the field of ever proliferating theory I had yet to seriously engage with the work of Benjamin.

*Dr Sean Homer*
*University of Sheffield*

**Gerhard Fischer (ed.)**, *With the Sharpened Axe of Reason: Approaches to Walter Benjamin* (Berg, Oxford), ISBN 1-85973-054-X, £14.99 pbk.

Marx on the commodity form: 'It is nothing but the definite relation between men themselves which assumes here, for them, the fantastic form of a relation between things.'

Carlyle on money: 'A human being who has worked with human beings clears all scores with them, cuts himself with triumphant completeness forever loose from them, by paying down certain shillings and pounds. Was it not the wages I promised you?'

Susan Buck-Morss, Benjamin scholar, in a recent discussion following a typically bracing lecture at the ICA, tried out an idea which had 'gone down well' with other audiences, wondering if we were nowadays witnessing 'the end of the commodity era' itself. The evidence she adduced, in this passing moment of debate, was her opinion that Americans are losing interest in their cars as status symbols. Extracting my rather expensive tape of the ICA event, I was struck by the irony of such a thesis. Theodor Adorno, a severe critic of many aspects of Benjamin's thinking, enthusiastically welcomed his protégé's attempts to translate the theological category of a materially corrupt world into the Marxist category of the commodity fetish. He worried that the quasi-revolutionary *homme de lettres* erred in the direction of conceiving commodity fetishism solely as a matter of consciousness. What might be immeasurably gained from emphasising those aspects of the struggle for emancipation which had fallen victim to a narrow preoccupation with 'socio-economic determinants', would be lost, if Benjamin neglected their material production.

What either of them would have made of this crudely empirical sleight of hand, waving the entire category into historical redundancy, is hard to imagine. But turn again to any vigorous eighteenth or nineteenth century text on commodity fetishism, investigating the breadth of the new concept's possible applications — the Romantic poets, Charles Dickens, Adam Smith and Adam Ferguson, alongside Thomas Carlyle and Karl Marx — and you revisit its relevance to today.

Why single out the ICA as a highly successful commodifier of intellectual production? It was with a similar sense of irony that I read *With the Sharpened Axe of Reason: Approaches to Walter Benjamin*. These lectures were mostly delivered at an international conference which was held at the University of New South Wales in Sydney and commemorated the centenary of Benjamin's birth. Some have been published in academic journals in Australia and Germany. The editor's preface hopes they will make a modest contribution to what he explicitly describes as 'the Benjamin industry that has come into existence since the 1970s', making the works of this 'unlikely guru ... prescribed reading in university courses around the world'.

Alarm bells start ringing when the attempt to offer some cohesive purpose for the anthology is abandoned in response to the nature of Benjamin's work itself — 'that peculiar and sometimes frustratingly puzzling mixture of aphorism and paradox, allegory and fragment', etc. The book's contents are therefore justified on the basis that the 'contributors' interdisciplinary interests and wide-ranging research questions reflect the plurality of Benjaminian discourses'. Another rhetorical flourish sounds further warning. These essays will avoid the 'empathy' of the 'adulatory-identificatory approach', in favour of providing 'decidedly critical perspectives' — where 'critical' holds none of the predictable resonances in coming to grips with this most dialectical of German cultural philosophers, but more of a stout Anglo-Saxon attempt to be detached, even unimpressed. What then is on offer?

In two essays, Benjamin is slapped on the wrists: 'The Essential Vulgarity of Benjamin's Essay on Goethe's *Elective Affinities*' and 'The Messiah Complex', where he is taken to task, with post-Stalinist hindsight, for a Utopian fixation with 'time travel', distracting him from the 'road of the present (which is in need of our critique)'. More troubling are essays clearly driven by the aforementioned research priorities of the contributors. David Roberts tries to 'substitute nature for the work of art' in Benjamin's famous essay on the 'Age of Mechanical Reproduction' in order to demonstrate the great distance between the interests of Critical Theory and contemporary ecological concerns. This is a contortion which does not yield worthwhile results. Similarly, three essays influenced by feminist criticism: John Docker's study of Benjamin on mass culture, and Sigrid Weigel on Benjamin and the modern city, compare him respectively and not usefully with the Leavises and Italo Calvino. But Margaret Mahony Stoljar's conclusion that Benjamin's use of gender images in the 'Arcades Project' extinguishes the 'woman reader's ability to engage with the text', is surely an example of thoroughly wrongheaded academic opportunism. She might look at the city-street scenes in Virginia Woolf's *Night and Day*. At any rate, she should not deter readers from enjoying this life-time's study of Paris as the dream capital of fashion and commodified desire.

Seeking contemporary relevance is of course a legitimate intellectual task, but this reluctant 'Benjamin-industry' bandwagon is immodest in assuming that whole sciences have 'moved on' since Benjamin's day. There are exceptions. Two chapters on Benjamin's neglected essay, 'Programme of a Proletarian Children's Theatre', do us a service by reintroducing these thoughts into our debates on alternative educational theory and practice. Two more contributions similarly relinquish any facile notion of historic progress: Michael Hollington traces tantalising filiations of influence between the nineteenth century Utopian thinker Charles Fourier, the French Surrealists, Walter Benjamin and Roland Barthes; David Frisby's 'methodological reflections' on the relevance of Walter Benjamin's work to the preoccupations of postmodernist analysis help us to understand Benjamin's continuity of thought. The latter is the sole essay one can recommend to a student as a helpmeet in reading Benjamin's difficult works. Its patience comes as a surprise in this volume. Of course, academic life has become more 'professionalised'. Academics are obsessed with research ratings and publication rates to get their funding. One can sympathise with people under such duress. However, Charles Leadbeater's assertion in a recent *New Statesman* that this 'dispersal of intellectual life', this breaking up of 'the old élite' is an unqualified good, seems purblind. Adorno's 1950s comments on the freedom of the intellectual come to mind,

Not only does the mind mould itself for the sake of its marketability, and thus reproduce the socially prevalent categories. Rather, it grows to resemble ever more closely the status quo even where it subjectively refrains from making a commodity of itself ... [It is cut off] a priori as it were from the possibility of differencing itself as all difference degenerates to a nuance in the monotony of supply ... Of its freedom it develops only the negative moment, irresponsibility. Otherwise, however, it clings ever more closely as a mere ornament to the material base which it aims to transcend.

Hence the irony, for if there is anything worth studying in Benjamin's tragically foreshortened life, it is his tortured bid to become a genuinely productive intellectual. Adorno once rebuked Benjamin for forgetting Lenin's critique of 'spontaneism' — which consigned the working class to darkness without the help of revolutionary intellectuals. Benjamin replied that 'political commitment, however revolutionary it may seem, functions in a counter-revolutionary way so long as the writer experiences his solidarity with the proletariat only in the mind and not as a producer': a more thought-provoking critique of 'empathy' than any you will find in this book of essays.

*Rosemary Bechler*
*Editor of* New Times

## The Contest for Social Science

**Eileen Janes Yeo**, *The Contest for Social Science: Relations and representations of gender and class* (Rivers Oram Press, London, 1996), ISBN 1-85489-068-9, 400pp., £30.00 hbk.

Did you know that William Wilberforce, early-1800s MP, anti-slavery campaigner, and prime mover in the Society For Bettering The Condition Of The Poor, kept a statistical table which tracked the state of his soul? One January day, for example, he felt he 'squandered' half-an-hour, whilst by contrast he spent three times as long consumed in 'Serious reading and meditation'. (p.6) Thus he marked out the lesser or greater moral turpitude of his days.

An Evangelical Anglican, and as such in the moral vanguard of the ruling classes, it is no surprise that Wilberforce was amongst those who fostered the newly-emergent 'science of managing the poor'. Philanthropic wisdom had begun to favour the inculcation of 'obedience, industry, prudence, foresight, virtue and cleanliness' as a condition of almsgiving. (p.81) Thus, the categories of value endorsed by Wilberforce and the like were foisted upon an initially unwitting, yet materially needy working-class.

And so it has continued, argues Eileen Janes Yeo in her ambitious and painstakingly researched new book, *The Contest for Social Science*. Yeo's subject matter is the ever-unceasing struggle for power between classes, and between men and women, as it has manifested itself in the practice of social science — literacy, the science of social improvement — and more recently in the preoccupations of sociologists and historians.

## Bettering society?

From the mid-eighteenth century working-class people were engaged in a constant battle with middle-class do-gooders. They desired change on their own terms, of course, and set up libraries and educational establishments. That way they could think about the best ways to achieve liberation, free from middle-class interference.

But what chance did they stand in the face of would-be professionals like lawyers and doctors, quick to hop on to the nineteenth-century 'science' bandwagon? Those earning a newly respectable living carried out statistical surveys in working-class areas with the intention of identifying and then eliminating the social 'problems' — illegitimacy, delinquency, crime — that they observed. But whilst these middle-class men were imbued with the highest sense of moral purpose — they subscribed to an ethic of public service — their 'social science' survey activities had the primary effect of consolidating their own social status. The poor, by comparison, were constructed as nothing but trouble.

The mid-nineteenth century also saw the emergence of a discourse of 'social motherhood' as middle-class women attempted to expand their public role. Social scientists at ground level, these women looked askance at the social and material conditions of the urban poor, piled one atop the other in filthy dwellings. What's more, they were prepared to get their hands dirty in the course of their attempts to help out — forming the nineteenth-century equivalent of housing associations, for example, and dispensing health education advice on visits to poor families. Their efforts were often reviled, and no wonder. Like Wilberforce and his Bettering Society, these philanthropic ladies unloaded middle-class morals along with the material assistance and educational opportunities that they offered to the objects of their reforming zeal.

In the twentieth century 'social science' has been absorbed by the state.

Health visitors, social workers, housing inspectors — all these occupations find their ancestry in the science of social improvement. Meanwhile, says Yeo, social theory lives on in a university Sociology Department near you.

## The contest for knowledge

Of necessity, *The Contest for Social Science* is a broad sweep, opening two hundred years ago in the wake of the French Revolution and closing in the contemporary academy. But it is also a well-detailed and closely argued piece of research, in which Yeo blends feminist theory and Marxist historiography with an invigorating dash of post-structuralism to produce a very palatable cultural studies-type account. Importantly, her text is more or less devoid of references to Foucault and his ilk, although she acknowledges her epistemological debts in the 'Introduction'; instead her book is loaded with illuminating primary sources.

At the same time *The Contest for Social Science* is a testimony to good planning. Whilst it moves chronologically through ten chapters, it develops thematically too. Once or twice it is repetitive, yes, where the exigencies of her giant remit force Yeo to cover ground she has already trodden. But this is a very small gripe in the face of what is an immensely complex and still utterly coherent study.

## The metaphor of social control

*The Contest for Social Science* is at its most persuasive where Yeo turns to metaphor to reinforce her arguments. In a chapter 'Body Metaphor in Social Science 1850–1930', which opens the book's third and final section 'Twentieth Century Directions', Yeo presents a literary interpretation of the polemics of that period. Drawing on the writings of the great and the good she demonstrates, for example, how the poorest of the poor, who were reputed to live surrounded by excrement, became as excrement in the literature of the day. What was needed, claimed society's self-nominated improvers was a kind of moral sewerage, which would flush away unwanted social elements.

For all Yeo's careful historicism, it is this turn to culture which clinches her case. The metaphors employed by Victorian social reformers carry with them a shock of recognition and an immediate line of descent for a more contemporary phraseology — 'white trash', 'ethnic cleansing' and so on. In this part of Yeo's narrative, the cultural politics of the late-nineteenth and early-twentieth century unfurl with a clatter, like a child's Jacob's Ladder, to resonate with ongoing debates on social rectification.

## Keep on keeping on

Latterly a community activist as well as an academic — and therefore both inside the academy and without — Yeo is particularly well-placed to chart the post-Enlightenment institutionalisation of social and political thought. But her own feet-in-two-camps position reflects the difficulty of pronouncing on what is never quite cut and dried. Even now, the middle-classes have not won and the working-classes have not lost and women push ahead, marking out more space for themselves. Yeo rightly credits socialism and feminism here, pointing to community publishing ventures, and feminist research initiatives, which continue to contest power and knowledge from below.

## The Yeo commandments

In the last pages of her text, Yeo issues a manifesto for academics — the late twentieth century's professionalised keepers of knowledge. Her instructions are as follows: first, research must allow its objects to speak, or to represent themselves, and this must be a legitimate part of any study second, the hierarchy of university and non-university knowledges must be dismantled, and third, social science research must always state its partiality, recognising that rational knowledge is power.

You have been told.

*Karen Triggs*
*Karen Triggs teaches Sociology and Politics at the University of East London*

# The Democracy of the Agents Themselves

**Colin Barker and Paul Kennedy (eds)**, *To Make Another World: Studies in protest and collective action* (Avebury Press, Aldershot, 1996), ISBN 1-85972-326-8, ix + 236pp., £35.00 hbk.

Despite a wealth of research in various corners of the academy geared towards the themes and theories of social movements (Marxist and feminist work being the most obvious examples), there is relatively little institutional space in these islands for discussion between those directly researching the different movements themselves. Manchester Metropolitan University's annual 'Alternative Futures and Popular Protest' conferences are therefore a welcome contribution to this dialogue, paralleling the political dialogue between contemporary movements (for example, the work of the Red-Green Study Group).

This collection of ten papers from the 1995 conference (plus introduction) covers a somewhat different spectrum of concerns and perspectives than American or continental 'social movement' agendas, particularly in its strong representation of class movements and Marxist perspectives. Other areas covered include the women's movement and feminism (Sue Clegg), the green-alternative movement (Paul Kennedy on green marketing and Jonathan Purkis on Earth First!), German deserters and revolutionaries from 1917–20 (Nick Howard) and what for me was one of the highlights of the book, an ethnographic account of how the London police handle demonstrations (Pat Waddington).

The papers are generally of high quality, but the sense of interaction between them is underdeveloped, with the exception of the Marxist critique of 'new social movement' theories; hopefully future publications will bring a greater engagement with alternative points of view. As Chik Collins writes of discourse analysis, in his piece on language use during the 1971–2 Clydeside work-in: 'The point is not to concede but to contest'. (p.86)

## Movements and intellectuals

The analogy and interaction between theoretical and 'directive' intellectual activity is central to any critical reflection on social movements, both in Marxist, feminist and other critical epistemologies which see knowledge as active relation and situated perspective, and in theorising the role of intellectual activity itself. Academic issues of method (how do we do research, what perspective do we adopt, what sort of knowledge do we think we are producing) are related to political issues of strategy and organisation. This is brought out well in Colin Barker's comparison of a 'professional' and a 'participatory' campaign to save a Manchester hospital, and in Alan Johnson's analysis of the weaknesses of Militant's strategy of 'mobilisation without participation' in Liverpool. There is a close relationship between intellectual analysis of the situation, the strategies adopted in research or organisation, and the 'response' of ordinary participants.

Most of the contributions, whether explicitly ethnographic or not, adopt the perspective of movement organisers, which gives this collection a greater sense of closeness to its subject matter than much 'social movement' literature. This can also be a weakness, if movements are identified with movement organisations at the expense of a broader sense of movement as class-for-itself, or its analogues in lived culture and social networks. The activity of organisers is itself of course geared to the wider movement, whose relationships and meanings they articulate; they are successful as movement intellectuals insofar as their thought and action is adequate to the broader reality of the movement. At the same time, the explicit and tangible nature of movement organisations makes them of interest to researchers as a source of knowledge of the whole movement.

This collection covers the spectrum of relationships implied by this analysis. A couple of pieces stress organisational strategy and the role of activists almost to the exclusion of anything else (Hamlet without the Prince of Denmark). The bulk of the contributions, however, do engage with the issue by relating the strategies of movement organisations and activists to the nature, creative activity, or potential of the movement 'basis': Gareth Dale's analysis of the conflict between participants and leaders in the East German movement of 1989 is a good example. Among the discussions of movements in the broader sense, Paul Bagguley's challenging piece sets out to examine the 'moral economy' underlying anti-poll tax protest. Tellingly, it relies on interviews with activists from the anti- poll tax unions to get at this.

## Time for reflexivity?

The relationship between intellectuals and movements is thus a key question; for those writing about contemporary movements in particular, it is also a reflexive one: how do we see our own role as critics, interpreters, ideologues or organisers in relation to the overall movement? The sources and nature of our own critical perspectives are implicated, as Clegg writes in her account of the relationship between the women's movement and feminist theory:

'Feminism, like any other set of theories which purports to serve and connect to a particular social movement, claims a specific relationship to praxis. There is a double linkage: a sociology of knowledge which looks at links between the movement and the development of ideas, and an epistemology which looks at the knowledge claims made by the movement.'(p. 46)

It is telling that hers is the only paper to seriously attempt the reflexive analysis of locating the production of theoretical knowledge — and the activities of critical intellectuals — in relation to the development of social movements. Writers on class and environmental movements still have much to learn from feminist analysis.

At the end of the book, however, what remains is the inspiration of reading so many reminders of the everyday possibility of creative resistance in what are mostly ordinary, contemporary contexts. As one of Barker's interviewees comments: 'I mean everything that we say about people is true. And even though you know it, you need reminding of it. But it's absolutely true. The creativeness, what people can do, all that, is all there'. (p.39)

*Laurence Cox*
*Laurence Cox is at Waterford Institute of Technology, Ireland. A report on the recent 'Alternative Cultures and Popular Protest' conference will appear in the next issue of* Socialist History

## Valiant-for-truth

Peter Gathercole, T.H. Irving and Gregory Melleuish (eds), *Childe and Australia: Archaeology, politics and ideas* (University of Queensland Press, St. Lucia, Queensland, 1995), ISBN 0-7022-2613-0, xxi + 245pp., $AUS29.95 hbk.

Australian-born Vere Gordon Childe (1892–1957) is well remembered and widely respected in Britain as a sensitive, detached, museum-oriented prehistorian of committed socialist persuasion. This was not always the case.

Educated at a Sydney Grammar School, at the University of Sydney, and at Queen's College, Oxford (1914–17), on his return to Australia Childe was blocked by academic conservatives from any hope of university employment. An active member of the Australian Labor Party, from 1919 to 1921 he served John Storey, New South Wales premier, as his Private Secretary and Research Officer. *How Labor Governs* (1924) reflects Childe's experience and critical understanding of ALP government in that period.

From 1922 Childe travelled widely in Central and Eastern Europe, and in 1925 he published *The Dawn of European Civilisation*, followed in 1926 by *The Aryans. From 1927 to 1946* he was professor of prehistoric archaeology at Edinburgh University, achieving fame (and exciting controversy) for his archaeological investigations at Skara Brae and on Rousay and Sanday in Orkney.

From 1946 to 1956 he was professor of prehistoric European archaeology at London University and director of its postgraduate Institute of

Archaeology. In these years he was a target for the political malevolence and harassment unleashed by the unsavoury United States senator, Joseph McCarthy, a strident echo of the political persecution Childe had earlier suffered in New South Wales and Queensland. As one of his students I recall with admiration his courage, and with gratitude his empathy with and support for those of us who endured like problems.

There is a considerable literature on the life and work of V. Gordon Childe, by P. Gathercole, S. Green (1981), T.H. Irving, B. McNairn (1980), G. Melleuish, W.J. Peace, A. Sherratt, B.C. Trigger (1980), B. Wailes (ed.) (1996) and others. *Childe and Australia* is a symposium originating from the V. Gordon Childe Centenary Conferenc at the University of Queensland, September 1990 under the auspices of the Australian Studies Centre.

Fourteen meticulously researched essays by thirteen scholars focus on Childe's life in Australia, his intellectual development, and his diverse achievements in social and archaeological theory and in Labour and Social Democratic politics.

Fifteen of Childe's private letters are included, addressed between 1917 and 1957 to friends and colleagues such as Raymond G. Watt, Gilbert Murray, S.J. Carruthers, Father O'Reilly, P.R. Stephenson, Reg Byrne, J.L. Myres, R. Palme Dutt, Mary Alice Evatt, John Morris, and O.G.S. Crawford. This correspondence illuminates the civil libertarian basis for Childe's opposition to the First World War; his energetic response to Sydney University's discrimination against him; his Labor activism in Queensland; his 1931 view of British politics ('I and everyone are thoroughly sick of MacDonald and Co. But there is no alternative less bad, the C.P. being quite hopeless here. We become a political agnostic.'). A poignant extract from his last testament of October 1957 declares: 'I have lost faith in all my old ideals.' and concludes: 'Life ends best when one is happy and strong.' Childe died, tragically, soon after.

The essays in this admirable collection are scholarly and intellectually challenging, often unveiling hidden aspects of Childe's complex personal character and of the theoretical hesitations and contradictions in his intellectual achievement. Several essays merit special notice. T.H. Irving outlines Childe's plans for a second volume of *How Labor Governs*; Peter Gathercole dissects the relationship between Childe's political and academic thought — and practice; William J. Peace analyses Childe's attitude to and vicissitudes in the Cold War; while Gregory Melleuish, Peter Beilharz and Tim Murray each provide retrospective chapters on aspects of Childe's contribution to Australian intellectual life, social theory, and archaeology respectively.

Barry Hindess on 'Sources of disillusion in Labour and Social

Democratic politics' (pp.183–98) subjects *How Labor Governs* to incisive analysis, stressing that the topic of socialist disillusion has an obvious bearing on the contemporary situation in several capitalist democracies, notably Blair's New Britain. Hindess considers what aspects of socialist doctrines and the political organisations to which they give rise are responsible for such disillusion, and addresses conceptual problems implicit in the construction of socialist doctrines.

Hindess concludes: 'Political idealism, disillusion and persistent conflicts between (unprincipled) realism and (unrealistic) utopianism will be with us for the foreseeable future.' In his view this is 'because an over-simple model of motivation and a notoriously imprecise notion of political realism continue to play an important part in the way we think about politics.'

This symposium is jam-packed with little known facts, sober political and ideological discussion, and sometimes startling insights with regard to intellectual and personal freedoms, and to those who seek to curtail them. William J. Peace's account of the making, reception and publishing record of Childe's *History* (1947) is specially enlightening.

Despite its firmly endorsing Marxist historiography, this book was critically discussed by Marxist historians in Britain. Seven reviews appeared in publications such as *Modern Quarterly* and *Labour Monthly*. Only one review appeared in America. In the US, Childe's dispassionate study was condemned as 'dangerous propaganda', and as 'a cheap piece of deception'. *History* has outlived all its critics, and is still seminal and stimulating.

Twenty-five pages of erudite notes, a useful reading list of biographical references and a competent, detailed index enhance the considerable academic importance of this first-rate, ground-breaking symposium, searching the early years of an enigmatic scholar whom political reactionaries pilloried and some British prehistorians caricatured.

Gordon Childe has emerged from this book with his reputation enhanced and his personality better understood. His later British career in prehistory obviously cannot be divorced from those thirty formative Australian years, or from his searing experience of social and academic intolerance.' (D.J. Mulvaney). Much more remains to be explored, but here we have a trustworthy sketch of the routes to be followed.

*H.G.A. Hughes*

# Books Received

Reviews of some of the following items are in preparation and will appear in future issues of the journal. Publishers sending items to be considered for review, and readers interested in reviewing any of the publications listed here, should write to Mike Waite, Socialist History reviews editor, c/o Burnley College, Higher Education Centre, School Lane, Burnley, BB11 1UF.

Readers considering submitting articles other than reviews, or sending general correspondence, should write to the Socialist History editorial team c/o Willie Thompson, Glasgow Caledonian University, Dept of Social Sciences, Cowcaddens Road, GLASGOW, G4 OBA.

Terrell Carver, *The Postmodern Marx* (Manchester University Press, Manchester, 1998), viii + 243 pp., ISBN 0-7190-4919-9, £12.99 pbk.

Andy Croft (ed.), *A Weapon in the Struggle: The cultural history of the Communist Party in Britain* (Pluto Press, London, 1998), vi + 218 pp., ISBN 0-7453-1204-7, £14.99 pbk.

Ralph Darlington, *The Political Trajectory of J.T. Murphy* (Liverpool University Press, Liverpool, 1998), xxx + 316pp., ISBN 0-8532-3743-3, £12.95 pbk.

Christopher Hill, *England's Turning Point: essays on seventeenth century English history* (Bookmarks, London, 1998), 366pp., ISBN 1-8988-7626-6, £12.99 pbk.

Jill Liddington, *Female Fortune: Land, gender and authority, The Anne Lister diaries and other writings 1833–1836* (Rivers Oram Press, London, 1998), xxi + 298pp., ISBN 1-85489-088-3 £35.00 hbk., ISBN 1-85489-089-1, £12.95 pbk.

David MacGregor, *Hegel and Marx after the fall of Communism* (University of Wales, Cardiff, 1998), xviii + 246pp., ISBN 0-70831-430-9, £12.95 pbk.

David Margolies, *Writing the Revolution: cultural criticism from Left Review* (Pluto Press, London, 1998), ix + 208pp., ISBN 0-7453-1162-8, £12.99 pbk.

Molly Murphy, with an Introduction by Ralph Darlington, *Suffragette and Socialist* (Institute for Social Research, University of Salford, 1998), viii + 168pp., ISBN 0-9044-8325-8, £7.99 pbk.

Edward Royle, *Robert Owen and the Conmencenent of the Millennium: A study of the Harmony community* (Manchester University Press, Manchester, 1998), ix + 274pp., ISBN 0-7190-5426-5, £45.00 hbk.

# Correspondence

*7 Hambledon House*
*Cricketfield Road*
*London E5 8NT*
*Tel 0181 985 2090 Fax 0181 533 5821*

I am reaching the final stages of work on a bibliography of the Communist Party of Great Britain and I wonder if any of your readers could help me trace items I may have missed. The bibliography will list all items published for sale by the CP nationally and locally (pamphlets, papers etc.) plus the *Daily Worker* and *Morning Star*, and the Young Communist League, together with theses and unpublished biographies or autobiographies. It will also include a comprehensive list of books, pamphlets and articles (except from daily and weekly papers) about the party.

If any reader is aware of any private collection or lesser known library collections that may contain such items I would be grateful if they could contact me. I am particularly keen to trace newsletters, journals and pamphlets produced by local branches and districts as these are harder to find than national ones.

*Yours sincerely*
*Dave Cope*

*Department of Government*
*University of Manchester*

A friend has recently drawn my attention to the report by David Morgan (issue 10, pp.80–1) of a one-day conference at Manchester in February 1996 on recent findings from the Moscow archives. The report includes a section on my introductory presentation at the conference. The following number of the journal (pp.125–6) contains a rebuttal from Robert Conquest which takes issue with my views, as presented by Morgan, on Stalin's moral responsibility for the famine of 1933.

In my presentation I showed that recent archival work would seem to suggest that Conquest has overstated the amount of grain reserves in 1933. In an article in *The Times Literary Supplement* on 11 February 1994 Conquest put the figure at 4.53 million tons whereas in his letter to your journal he revises the figure downwards to about 3 million tons. The source which I quoted at the conference suggested, by contrast, that the total amount of grain set aside in reserve stocks amounted to about 1.41 million tons on 1 July 1933 (R.W. Davies, M.B. Tauger and S.G. Wheatcroft, 'Stalin, Grain Stocks and the Famine of 1932–1933', *Slavic Review*, vol.54, no.3: 656)

My quarrel, however, is far less with Robert Conquest than it is with David Morgan's wanton misrepresentation of my views. At no point did I say, as Morgan claims, that 'the assertion that Stalin deliberately held back grain to engineer famine in 1932 is finally disproved by economic figures showing that there were no extra grain reserves available in the country' and that 'thus the famine was not a creation of a bureaucratic decree but a natural phenomenon'. The balance of evidence suggests, on the contrary, that the Soviet regime could considerably have mitigated the effects of the famine. As the article by Davies *et al.*, puts it: 'it seems certain that, if Stalin had risked lower levels of these reserves in spring and summer 1933, hundreds of thousands —perhaps millions — of lives could have been saved.' (p.657) There is little doubt that Stalin prioritized the goals of his Five Year Plans over the needs of peasants, Ukrainians among them. Here, as in so many other areas, Stalin showed a monstrous disregard for human life.

[The author concludes with a point regarding the handling of the report which we have responded to in private correspondence.]

*Yours faithfully*
*Yoram Gorlizki*

*44 Coolhurst Road,*
*London N8 8EU*

May I comment on the article on the Communist Party Historian's Group by David Parker in your issue No.12 which I found extremely interesting and informative? I am puzzled however by the omission of the earliest years of the Group — perhaps because its meetings were informal and there are no minutes recorded. The group was inspired by Dona Torr, who is not even mentioned (nor is her work on Tom Mann), and Christopher Hill. I recall an early meeting in which we expressed our disgust with a review by Andrew Rothstein in the *Labour Monthly* of his book.

Then there is no mention of the fact that the earliest publications inspired by the Group were the series 'History in the Making' (General Editor, Dona Torr). The first volume of which by myself, *From Cobbett to the Chartists*, was published in 1948, with a second, hardback edition and a German translation in 1951. This was followed by a book on the mid century by James Jeffries and later by a volume on the late-nineteenth century by Eric Hobsbawn. There was also a volume on the late eighteenth century, and of course *The Good Old Cause*, by Christopher Hill and Edmund Dell on the seventeenth century.

I ceased to be a member of the Group in the very early 1950s. The British Museum authorities wrongly informed me when I returned from India in 1946 that the Newspaper Repository in Colindale, which had been bombed, would not be available for eight years. Whereupon I ceased to be a historian, as the Colindale records were essential for a biography I was writing of Bronterre O'Brien. *From Cobbett to the Chartists* derived from such prewar reading and notes as I had made.

May I record the very happy atmosphere of the early years of the then rather small Group which I recall with great pleasure.

*Yours fraternally,*
*Max Morris*

**Rivers Oram Titles of Related Interest**

**Digging Up Trouble**
*The environment, protest and open-cast mining*
*Huw Beynon, Andrew Cox and Ray Hudson*

This book examines the complex subject of environmental planning in relation to broader concerns of political economy and local culture. It presents the words and actions of local people, politicians, planners and industrialists in a way which allows the reader to understand and analyse the different interests and perceptions which bear upon local planning decisions. It confronts the world of 'common sense' with that of 'the expert' and raises questions about knowledge, and how this relates to political and economic decision making.

This original and detailed account invites a consideration of both contemporary values, and of the significance of landscape and place in everyday life.

Huw Beynon is director of the ESRC Research Centre on Innovation and Competition at the University of Manchester. Andrew Cox is editor of UK *Coal Review*. Ray Hudson is Professor of Geography, Director of the Centre of European Studies at Durham and a director of the ESRC Resource Centre for Access to Data on Europe.

*Publication July 1999*
*288pp 234x156mm*
*ISBN 1 85489 112 X (hb) £35.00*
*ISBN 1 85489 113 8 (pb) £14.95*

## The Contest for Social Science
*Relations and representations of gender and class*
Eileen Janes Yeo

Opening in the period of revolutions between 1789 and 1850, this book looks at the contention over social science from above and below. It breaks away from orthodox interpretations of the development of social science to explore the subject as a contest for class and gender power.

...breaks into exciting new ground — *History Today*

One of the best analyses of the development of the social sciences ... it is a 'must' for all students of social policy, sociology and history. This book is a stunner. — *Labour History Review*

... a richly textured, multi-layered, and theoretically sophisticated analysis of the development of social science ... Yeo's discussion of the intersections and interweaving of gender and class is admirable, and her demonstration of the power of language as well as the power of hierarchical relations in shaping the development of social science is much to be admired ... the empirical analysis and wide-ranging nature of this book make it a stellar example of contemporary social/cultural history. — *International Review of Social History*

This book will be generating discussion within sociology, social work, women's studies, cultural studies, the sociology of knowledge, and the other social sciences for many years to come. — *Sociology*

*424pp 216x138mm*
*ISBN 1 85489 068 9 (hb) £30.00*

## Mary Wollstonecraft and 200 Years of Feminisms
*Eileen Janes Yeo (editor)*

To mark the 200th anniversary of Mary Wollstonecraft's death, this book brings together contributions which capture important and continuing moments in feminist scholarship from all over the world. Covering interdisciplinary readings of Wollstonecraft's texts to historical explorations of the politics of gender, they reflect a convergence of feminist theory and practice. The contributors include: Moira Ferguson, Joan Landes, Mary Nyquist, Joan Wallach Scott and Barbara Taylor.

Eileen Janes Yeo was educated at Brandeis and the University of Wisconsin. She teaches history at the University of Sussex.

*288 pp 234x150mm*
*ISBN 1 85489 060 3 (hb) £30.00*
*ISBN 1 85489 061 1 (pb) £12.95*

## JOIN THE SOCIALIST HISTORY SOCIETY

Membership entitles you to attend all the Society's events, to receive two numbers of *Socialist History* per year plus two pamphlets, and to participate in its decision making.

*Subscription rates are:*
£17.50 waged (£22.50 overseas);
£10.00 unwaged (£15.00 overseas);
£20.00 labour movement organisations


Willie Thompson
Division of History
Department of Social Sciences
Glasgow Caledonian University
Glasgow G4 0BA

Tel:     +44 141-331 3253
Fax:    +44 141 331 3439

e-mail: w.thompson@gcal.ac.uk